Workshop on Domain Adaptation for Natural Language Processing 2010

(DANLP 2010)

Held at ACL 2010

Uppsala, Sweden
15 July 2010

ISBN: 978-1-61738-815-6

Printed from e-media with permission by:

Curran Associates, Inc.
57 Morehouse Lane
Red Hook, NY 12571

Some format issues inherent in the e-media version may also appear in this print version.

Printed by Curran Associates, Inc. (2010)

For permission requests, please contact the Association for Computational Linguistics
at the address below.

Association for Computational Linguistics
209 N. Eighth Street
Stroudsburg, Pennsylvania 18360

Phone: 1-570-476-8006
Fax: 1-570-476-0860

acl@aclweb.org

Additional copies of this publication are available from:

Curran Associates, Inc.
57 Morehouse Lane
Red Hook, NY 12571 USA
Phone: 845-758-0400
Fax: 845-758-2634
Email: curran@proceedings.com
Web: www.proceedings.com

Preface

Most modern Natural Language Processing (NLP) systems are subject to the well known problem of lack of portability to new domains and genres: there is a substantial drop in their performance when tested on data from a new domain, i.e., when test data is drawn from a related but different distribution from training data. This problem is inherent in the assumption of independent and identically distributed (i.i.d.) variables for machine learning systems, but has started to get attention only in recent years. The need for domain adaptation arises in almost all NLP tasks – the goal of this workshop is to provide a meeting point for research that approaches the problem of adaptation from the varied perspectives of machine learning and a variety of NLP tasks. We believe there is much to gain by treating domain adaptation as a general learning strategy that utilizes prior knowledge of a specific or a general domain in learning about a new domain. Sharing insights, methodologies and successes across tasks will contribute towards a better understanding of this problem. To this end, this workshop presents original research in areas such as parsing, machine translation, dialog act tagging, entity recognition, summarization, etc. with the common theme of domain adaptation. We received sixteen submissions in all, out of which eight were selected for inclusion in the workshop.

We thank the members of the Program Committee for timely and insightful reviews, and the invited speaker John Blitzer for his talk.

Hal Daumé III, Tejaswini Deoskar, David McClosky, Barbara Plank and Jörg Tiedemann

Organizers:

Hal Daumé III, University of Utah, USA
Tejaswini Deoskar, University of Amsterdam, The Netherlands
David McClosky, Stanford University, USA
Barbara Plank, University of Groningen, The Netherlands
Jörg Tiedemann, Uppsala University, Sweden

Program Committee:

Eneko Agirre, University of the Basque Country, Spain
John Blitzer, University of California, USA
Walter Daelemans, University of Antwerp, Belgium
Mark Dredze, Johns Hopkins University, USA
Philipp Koehn, University of Edinburgh, United Kingdom
Kevin Duh, NTT Communication Science Laboratories, Japan
Jing Jiang, Singapore Management University, Singapore
Oier Lopez de Lacalle, University of the Basque Country, Spain
Robert Malouf, San Diego State University, USA
Ray Mooney, University Texas, USA
Hwee Tou Ng, National University of Singapore, Singapore
Khalil Sima'an, University of Amsterdam, The Netherlands
Michel Simard, National Research Council of Canada, Canada
Jun'ichi Tsujii, University of Tokyo, Japan
Antal van den Bosch, Tilburg University, The Netherlands
Josef van Genabith, Dublin City University, Ireland
Yi Zhang, German Research Centre for Artificial Intelligence (DFKI GmbH) and Saarland University, Germany

Invited Speaker:

John Blitzer, University of California, USA

Table of Contents

Conference Program

Thursday 15 July 2010

9:15-9:30	Opening by Barbara Plank
9:30-10:30	Invited Talk "Semi-supervised Domain Adaptation: From Practice to Theory" by John Blitzer
10:30-11:00	Morning Break
	Session I:
11:00–11:25	*Adaptive Parameters for Entity Recognition with Perceptron HMMs* Massimiliano Ciaramita and Olivier Chapelle
11:30–11:55	*Context Adaptation in Statistical Machine Translation Using Models with Exponentially Decaying Cache* Jörg Tiedemann
12:00–12:25	*Domain Adaptation to Summarize Human Conversations* Oana Sandu, Giuseppe Carenini, Gabriel Murray and Raymond Ng
12:30-14:00	Lunch
	Session II:
14:00–14:25	*Exploring Representation-Learning Approaches to Domain Adaptation* Fei Huang and Alexander Yates
14:30–14:55	*Using Domain Similarity for Performance Estimation* Vincent Van Asch and Walter Daelemans
15:00–15:25	*Self-Training without Reranking for Parser Domain Adaptation and Its Impact on Semantic Role Labeling* Kenji Sagae
15:30-16:00	Afternoon Break

Thursday 15 July 2010 (continued)

Session III:

16:00–16:25 *Domain Adaptation with Unlabeled Data for Dialog Act Tagging*
Anna Margolis, Karen Livescu and Mari Ostendorf

16:30–16:55 *Frustratingly Easy Semi-Supervised Domain Adaptation*
Hal Daumé III, Abhishek Kumar and Avishek Saha

17:00-17:45 Panel Discussion by John Blitzer, Walter Daelemans, Hal Daumé III, Jing Jiang, Khalil Sima'an

Adaptive Parameters for Entity Recognition with Perceptron HMMs

Massimiliano Ciaramita[*]
Google
Zürich, Switzerland
massi@google.com

Olivier Chapelle
Yahoo! Research
Sunnyvale, CA, USA
chap@yahoo-inc.com

Abstract

We discuss the problem of model adaptation for the task of named entity recognition with respect to the variation of label distributions in data from different domains. We investigate an adaptive extension of the sequence perceptron, where the adaptive component includes parameters estimated from unlabelled data in combination with background knowledge in the form of gazetteers. We apply this idea empirically on adaptation experiments involving two newswire datasets from different domains and compare with other popular methods such as self training and structural correspondence learning.

1 Introduction

Model adaptation is a central problem in learning-based natural language processing. In the typical setting a model is trained on annotated *in domain*, or *source*, data, and is used on *out of domain*, or *target*, data. The main difference with respect to similar problems such as semi-supervised learning is that source and target data are not assumed to be drawn from the same distribution, which might actually differ in relevant distributional properties: topic, domain, genre, style, etc. In some formulations of the problem a few target labeled data is assumed to be available (Daumé III, 2007). However, we are interested in the case in which no labeled data is available from the target domain – except for evaluation purposes and fine tuning of hyperparameters.

Most of the work in adaptation has focused so far on the input side; e.g, proposing solutions based on generating shared source-target representations (Blitzer et al., 2006). Here we focus instead on the output aspect. We hypothesize that part of the loss incurred in using a model out of domain is due to its built-in class priors which do not match the class distribution in the target data. Thus we attempt to explicitly correct the prediction of a pre-trained model for a given label by taking into account a noisy estimate of the label frequency in the target data. The correction is carried out by means of adaptive parameters, estimated from unlabelled target data and background "world knowledge" in the form of gazetteers, and taken in consideration in the decoding phase. We built a suitable dataset for experimenting with different adaptation approaches for named entity recognition (NER). The main findings from our experiments are as follows. First, the problem is challenging and only marginal improvements are possible under all evaluated frameworks. Second, we found that our method compares well with current state-of-the-art approaches such as self training and structural correspondence learning (McClosky et al., 2006; Blitzer et al., 2006) and taps on an interesting aspect which seems worth of further research. Although we concentrate on a segmentation task within a specific framework, the perceptron HMM introduced by Collins (2002), we speculate that the same intuition could be straightforwardly applied in other learning frameworks (e.g., Support Vector Machines) and different tasks (e.g., standard classification).

2 Related work

Recent work in domain adaptation has focused on approaches such as *self-training* and *structural correspondence learning* (SCL). The former approach involves adding self-labeled data from the target domain produced by a model trained in-domain (McClosky et al., 2006). The latter approach focuses on ways of generating shared source-target representations based on good cross-domain (pivot) features (Blitzer et al., 2006) (see

[*]This work was carried out while the first author was working at Yahoo! Research Barcelona.

Proceedings of the 2010 Workshop on Domain Adaptation for Natural Language Processing, ACL 2010, pages 1–7,
Uppsala, Sweden, 15 July 2010.

also (Ando, 2004)). Self training has proved effective in syntactic parsing, particularly in tandem with discriminative re-ranking (Charniak and Johnson, 2005), while the SCL has been applied successfully to tasks such PoS tagging and opinion analysis (Blitzer et al., 2006; Blitzer et al., 2007). We address a different aspect of the adaptation problem, namely the difference in label distributions between source and target domains. Chan and Ng (2006) proposed correcting the class priors for domain adaptation purposes in a word sense disambiguation task. They adopt a generative framework where the base model is a naive Bayes classifier and priors are re-estimated with EM. The approach proposed by Chelba and Acero (2004) is also related as they propose a MAP adaptation via Gaussian priors of a MaxEnt model for recovering the correct capitalization of text.

Domain adaptation naturally invokes the existence of a specific task and data. As such it is natural to consider the modeling aspects within the context of a specific application. Here we focus on the problem of named entity recognition (NER). There is still little work on adaptation for NER. Ando (2004) reports successful experiments on adapting with an SCL-like approach, while Ciaramita and Altun (2005) effectively used external knowledge in the form of gazetteers in a semi-Markov model. Mika *et al.* (2008) used Wikipedia to generate additional training data for domain adaptation purposes.

3 Problem statement

Named entity taggers detect mentions of instances of pre-defined categories such as person (Per), location (Loc), organization (Org) and miscellaneous (Misc). The problem can be naturally framed as a segmentation and labeling task. State of the art systems, e.g., based on sequential optimization, achieve excellent accuracy in domain. However, accuracy degrades if the target data diverges in relevant distributional aspects from the source. As an example, the following is the output of a perceptron HMM[1] trained on the CoNLL 2003 English data (news) (Sang and Muelder, 2003) when applied to a molecular biology text:[2]

(1) [**Cdc2-cyclin**]^{Org} [**B-activated Polo-like**]^{Misc} kinase specifically phosphorylates at least three components of [**APC**]^{Org}.

The tagger predicts several CoNLL entities which are unlikely to occur in that context. One source of confusion is probably the shape of words, including case, numbers, and non alphabetical characters, which are also typical, and thus misleading, of unrelated CoNLL entities. However, we argue that the problem is partially due to the parameters learned which reflect the distribution of classes in the source data. The parameter, acting as biased priors, lead the tagger to generate inappropriate distributions of labels. We propose that this aspect of the problem might be alleviated by correcting the score for each class with an estimate of the class frequency in the target data. Thus, with respect to the example, we would like to decrease the score of "Org" labels according to their expected frequency in a molecular biology corpus.

4 A perceptron with adjustable priors

As generic taggers we adopt perceptron-trained HMMs (Collins, 2002) which have excellent efficiency/performance trade-off (Nguyen and Guo, 2007). The objective of learning is a discriminant $F : \mathcal{X} \times \mathcal{Y} \rightarrow \mathbb{R}$, where $\mathcal{Y}$ denotes sequences of labels from a pre-defined set of categories Y. $F(\mathbf{x}, \mathbf{y}; \alpha) = \langle \alpha, \Phi(\mathbf{x}, \mathbf{y}) \rangle$ is linear in a feature representation Φ defined over a joint input/output space,[3] a global feature representation mapping each $(\mathbf{x}, \mathbf{y})$ pair to a vector of feature counts $\Phi(\mathbf{x}, \mathbf{y}) \in \mathbb{R}^d$:

$$[\Phi(\mathbf{x}, \mathbf{y})]_i = \sum_{j=1}^{|\mathbf{y}|} \phi_i(y_{j-1}, y_j, \mathbf{x}), \qquad (2)$$

where ϕ_i is a (binary) predicate. Given an input sequence $\mathbf{x}$, we find the optimal label sequence, $f(\mathbf{x}; \alpha) = \arg\max_{\mathbf{y} \in \mathcal{Y}} F(\mathbf{x}, \mathbf{y}; \alpha)$, with Viterbi decoding. The model α is learned with the perceptron algorithm.

Each feature represents a spelling or contextual property, or the previous label. The simplest baseline (model B) uses the features listed in the upper half of Table 1. In previous work on NER adaptation, Ciaramita and Altun (2005) found that gazetteers, in combination with semi-Markov models, significantly improved adaptation. Similarly, we define additional features using

[1]We used the implementation available from `http://sourceforge.net/projects/supersensetag`, more details on this tagger can be found in (Ciaramita and Altun, 2006).

[2]The same model achieves F-scores well in excess of 90% evaluated in domain.

[3]$\langle \mathbf{u}, \mathbf{v} \rangle$ denoting the inner product between $\mathbf{u}$ and $\mathbf{v}$.

Model B features			
Feature	example token	feature value(s)	Position
Lowercase word	Pierre	pierre	*i-1, i, i+1*
Part of Speech	Pierre	NNP	*i-1, i, i+1*
Word Shape	Pierre	Xx	*i-1, i, i+1*
$\text{Suffix}_{2/3}$	Pierre	{re, rre}	*i*
$\text{Prefix}_{2/3}$	Pierre	{pi, pie}	*i*
Previous label	Vinken (in "Pierre Vinken")	B-PER (label on "Pierre")	*i*
Additional features of model BG			
Feature	example token	feature value(s)	Position
InGazetteer	Islands (in "Cayman Islands")	I-Country_2 (inside a 2-word country name)	*i-1, i, i+1*
Most frequent supersense	Eve	B-Per_1 (1 token Person label)	*i*
2 most frequent supersenses	Eve	B-Per-Time_1 (1 token Person/Time label)	*i*
Number of supersenses	Eve	B-NSS4_1	*i*

Table 1. Feature list and examples. The upper half lists the features for the baseline tagger (B), the lower half lists the additional features extracted from the gazetteers included to the second non-adapted tagger (BG). The last number on the feature indicates the length of the entry in the list; e.g., "Islands" in the example is the end of a two-word item, in the country gazetteer, because of "Cayman Islands". The remaining features capture the most frequent Wordnet supersense of the word, the first and second most frequent supersenses, and the total number of supersenses.

the gazetteers from GATE,[4] (Cunningham et al., 2002) namely, countries, person first/last names, trigger words; and also from Wordnet: using the lexicographers or *supersense* labels; and a list of company names from Fortune 500. For this second baseline (model BG) we also extract the features in the bottom half of Table 1.

4.1 Decoding with external priors

In our method training is performed on the source data using the perceptron algorithm. Adaptation takes place at decoding time, when the score of the entity labels is adjusted according to a k-dimensional parameter vector $\theta, k = |Y|$, estimated by comparing the source and the unlabeled target data. The score of a sequence $\hat{\mathbf{y}}$ for input $\mathbf{x}$ in the target domain is computed with a variant of the original discriminant:

$$F'(\mathbf{x}, \mathbf{y}; \alpha) = \sum_{j=1}^{|\mathbf{y}|} \left(\sum_{i=1}^{d} \phi_i(y_{j-1}, y_j, \mathbf{x})\alpha_i \right) + \tau\theta_{y_j} \quad (3)$$

where θ_{y_j} is the adaptive parameter associated with y_j, and τ is a scaling factor. The new prediction for $\mathbf{x}$ is $f'(\mathbf{x}; \alpha) = \arg\max_{\mathbf{y}\in\mathcal{Y}} F'(\mathbf{x}, \mathbf{y}; \alpha)$.

5 Adaptive parameters

5.1 Theta

The vector θ encodes information about the expected difference in frequency of each category between source and target. Let $g_Q(c) = \frac{\text{count}(c,Q)}{\sum_{c'} count(c',Q)}$ be an estimate of the relative frequency of class c in corpus Q. We propose to formulate θ_c as:

$$\theta_c = \frac{g_T(c) - g_S(c)}{g_S(c)} \quad (4)$$

where T and S are, respectively, the source and target data. This is the ratio of the difference between in and out domain relative frequencies for class c, with respect to the in domain frequency. Intuitively, $g_S(c)$ represents an estimate of the frequency of c in the source S, and θ_c an estimate of the expected decrease/increase as a fraction of the initial guess; θ_c is negative if class c is less frequent in the target data than in the source data, and positive otherwise. From this, it is clear that equation (3) will offset the scores in the desired direction.

A crucial issue is the estimation of $\text{count}(c, Q)$, a guess of the frequency of c in Q. A simple solution could be to count directly the class frequencies from the labeled source data, and to obtain a noisy estimate on the target data by counting the occurrence of entities that have known labels in the source data. This approach unfortunately works very badly for at least two reasons. First, the number of entities in each class reflects the frequency of the class in the source. Therefore using lists of entities from the source as proxies for the class in the target data can transfer the source bias to the target. Second, entities can have different senses in different domains; e.g., several English city names occur in the Wall Street Journal as locations (Liverpool, Manchester, etc.) and

[4]http://www.gate.ac.uk/.

Attribute	CoNLL	BBN-4
# tokens	300K	1.046M
Source	Reuters	Wall Street Journal
Domain	General news	Financial
Years	1992	1987
# entities	34,841	58,637
Loc	30.48%	22.51%
Per	28.58%	20.08%
Org	26.55%	46.27%
Misc	14.38%	10.41%

Table 2. BBN and CoNLL datasets.

in Reuters news as both locations and organizations (football clubs). We propose to use lists of words which are strongly associated with entities of specific classes but are extracted from an independent third source. In this way, we hope the bias they carry will be transferred in similar ways to both source and target. Similarly, potential ambiguities should be randomly distributed between source and target. Thus, as a first approximation, we propose that given a list of words L_c, supposedly related to c and generated independently from source and target, $\text{count}(c, Q)$ can be defined as:

$$\text{count}(c, Q) \equiv \sum_{w \in L_c} \text{count}(w, Q) \quad (5)$$

5.2 Tau

The scalar τ needs to be large enough to revise the decision of the base model, if necessary. However, τ should not be too large, otherwise the best prediction of the base model would be ignored. In order for τ to have an effective, but balanced, magnitude we introduce a simple notion of margin. Let the score of a given label y_s on token s be: $G(\mathbf{x}, y_s; \alpha) = \sum_{i=1}^{d} \phi_i(y_{s-1}, y_s, \mathbf{x})\alpha_i$, and let $\hat{y}_s = \arg\max_{y \in \mathcal{Y}} G(\mathbf{x}, y; \alpha)$, we define the margin on s as:

$$M_s \equiv \min_{y_s \neq \hat{y}_s} (G(\mathbf{x}, \hat{y}_s; \alpha) - G(\mathbf{x}, y_s; \alpha)). \quad (6)$$

The mean of M provides a rough quantification of the necessary amount by which we need to offset the scores $G(\mathbf{x}, y_s; \alpha)$ in order to change the predictions. As a first guess, we take $\tau = \mu(M_S) = \frac{1}{|S|} \sum_s^{|S|} M_s$, which we interpret as an upper bound on the desired value of τ. While experimenting on the development data we found that τ/2 yields good results.

6 Experimental setup

6.1 Data

We used two datasets for evaluation. The first is the English CoNLL 2003 dataset (Sang and Muelder, 2003), a corpus of Reuters news annotated with person, location, organization and miscellaneous entity tags. The second is the BBN corpus (BBN, 2005), which supplements the WSJ Penn TreeBank with annotation for 105 categories: named entities, nominal entities and numeric types. We made the two datasets "semantically" compatible as follows. We tagged a large collection of text from the English Wikipedia with CoNLL and BBN taggers. We counted the frequencies of BBN/CoNLL tag pairs for the same strings, and assigned each BBN tag the most frequent CoNLL tag;[5] e.g.,

BBN tag		CoNLL tag
Work_of_art:Book	→	Misc
Organization:Educational	→	Org
Location:Continent	→	Loc
Person	→	Per

48 BBN-to-CoNLL pairs were labelled in this way. Remaining categories, e.g., descriptive and numerical types, were mapped to the Outside tag as they are not marked in CoNLL. Finally, we substituted all tags in the BBN corpus with the corresponding CoNLL tag, we call this corpus BBN-4. The data is summarized in Table 2. Notice the different label distributions: the BBN-4 data is characterized by a skewed distribution of labels with organization by far the most frequent class, while the CoNLL data has a more uniform distribution with location as the most frequent class. The CoNLL data was randomly split in three disjoint sets of sentences for training (16,540 sentences), development (2.068) and test (2,136). For BBN-4 we used WSJ sections 2-21 for training (39,823), section 22 for development (1,700) and section 23 for test (2,416). We evaluated models in both directions; i.e., swapping CoNLL and BBN-4 as source/target.

6.2 Model tuning

We regularize the perceptrons by averaging (Freund and Schapire, 1999). The perceptron HMM

[5] A simpler approach might that of manually mapping the two tagsets, however a number of cases that are not trivial to resolve emerges in this way. For this reason we decided to adopt the described data-driven heuristic approach.

has only one hyper-parameter, the number of training iterations (or epochs). Models trained for application out of domain can benefit from early stopping which provides an additional mean of regularization. For all models compared we used the development sets for choosing the number of epochs for training the perceptron on the source data. This is an important step as different adaptation approaches yield different overfitting pattern and it is important to control for this factor for a fair comparison. As an example, we found that the self-training models consistently overfit after just a few iterations after which performance has a steep drop. The order of presentation of instances in the training algorithm is randomized; for each method we repeat the process 10 times and report average F-score and standard error.

The vector θ was estimated using one of the same gazetteers used in the base tagger (BG), a list of 1,438 *trigger words* from GATE.[6] These are words associated with certain categories; e.g., "abbess/Per", "academy/Org", "caves/Loc", and "manifesto/Misc". The lists for different classes contain varying numbers of items and might contain misleading words. To obtain more reliable estimates of comparable magnitude between classes we computed equation (4) several times by sampling an equal number of words from each list and taking the mean. On the development set this proved better than computing the counts from the entire list.

Other sources could be evaluated, for example lists of entities of each class extracted from Wikipedia. We used all single-word triggers: 191 for Loc, 171 for Misc, 89 for Org and 592 for Per. With each list we estimated θ as in Section 5.1 for each of the four labels starting with "B", i.e., entity beginnings, $\theta = 0$ for the other five labels. To find θ we use as source S, the in-domain data, and as target T the out-domain data. The lists contain different number of items and might contain misleading words.

To set τ we compute the mean margin (6) on CoNLL, using the tagger trained on CoNLL ($\mathrm{mean}(M_s) \approx 50$), similarly for BBN-4 ($\mathrm{mean}(M_s) \approx 38$). We used the development set to fine tune the adaptive rate setting it equal to $\tau = \frac{1}{2}\mathrm{mean}(M_s)$.

[6]This list corresponds to the list of words L_c of Section 5.1.

6.3 Self training

To compare with self-training we trained a tagger (BG) on the training set of CoNLL. With the tagger we annotated the training set of BBN-4, and added the self-labeled data, 39,823 BBN-4 sentences, to the gold standard CoNLL training. Similarly, in the reverse direction we trained a tagger (BG) on the training set of BBN-4, annotated the training set of CoNLL, and added the self-labeled 16,540 CoNLL sentences to the BBN-4 training. We denote these models BG_{SELF}, and the augmented sources as CoNLL+ and BBN-4+.

6.4 Structural correspondence learning

We first implemented a simple baseline following the idea presented in (Ando, 2004). The basic idea consists in performing an SVD decomposition of the feature-token matrix, where the matrix contains all the sentences from the source and target domains. The goal is to capture co-occurrences of features and derive new features which are more stable. More specifically, we extracted the 50 principal directions of the feature-token matrix and projected all the data onto these directions. This results in 50 new additional features for each token that we append to the original (sparse binary) feature vector ϕ_i, $1 \leq i \leq d$. In order to give equal importance to the original and new features, we multiplied the new features by a constant factor such that the average L_1 norms of the new and old features are the same. Note that this weighting might not be optimal but should be sufficient to detect if these new features are helpful or not.

We then implemented several versions of structural correspondence learning. First, following the original formulation (we refer to this model as SCL1), 100 *pivot* features are selected, these are frequent features in both source and target data. For a given pivot feature k, a vector $\mathbf{w}_k \in \mathbb{R}^d$ is computed by performing a regularized linear regression between all the other features and the given pivot feature. The matrix W whose columns are the $\mathbf{w}_k$ is formed and the original feature vectors are projected onto the 50 top left singular vectors of W, yielding 50 new features. We also tried the following variants. In the version we refer to as SCL2 we rescale the left singular vectors of W by their corresponding singular values. In the last variant (SCL3) we select the pivot features which are frequent in the source and target domains *and* which are also predictive for the task (as measured

Model	Source	Target	Test
B	BBN-4	CoNLL	60.4 $\pm$.28
BG	BBN-4	CoNLL	66.1 $\pm$.32
BG_{SVD}	BBN-4	CoNLL	66.5 $\pm$.26
BG_{SCL1}	BBN-4	CoNLL	66.8 $\pm$.18
BG_{SCL2}	BBN-4	CoNLL	64.7 $\pm$.24
BG_{SCL3}	BBN-4	CoNLL	66.8 $\pm$.27
BG_{SELF}	BBN-4+	CoNLL	65.5 $\pm$.26
BG_{θ}	BBN-4	CoNLL	66.8 $\pm$.53
Model	Source	Target	Test
B	CoNLL	BBN-4	65.0 $\pm$.77
BG	CoNLL	BBN-4	67.6 $\pm$.69
BG_{SVD}	CoNLL	BBN-4	67.9 $\pm$.54
BG_{SCL1}	CoNLL	BBN-4	67.9 $\pm$.45
BG_{SCL2}	CoNLL	BBN-4	68.1 $\pm$.53
BG_{SCL3}	CoNLL	BBN-4	67.8 $\pm$.34
BG_{SELF}	CoNLL+	BBN-4	68.3 $\pm$.36
BG_{θ}	CoNLL	BBN-4	70.3 $\pm$.61

Table 3. Results of baselines and adaptive models.

by the mutual information between the feature and the class label). The 50 additional features are appended to the original (sparse binary) feature vector ϕ_i, $1 \leq i \leq d$, and again, they are first rescaled in order to have the same average L_1 norm as the old features over the entire dataset.

7 Results and discussion

Table 3 summarizes the experimental results on both datasets. We refer to our adaptive model as BG_θ. Adapting a model from BBN-4 to CoNLL, self training (BG_{SELF}, 65.5%) performs slightly worse than the base model (BG, 66.1%). The best SCL model, the original formulation, produces a small, but likely significant, improvement (BG_{SCL1}, 66.8%). Our model (BG_θ, 66.8%), achieves the same result but with larger variance. The improvement of the best models over the first baseline (B, 60.4%) is considerable, +6.4%, but mostly due to gazetteers.

In the adaptation experiments from CoNLL to BBN-4 both self training (BG_{SELF}, 68.3%) and the best SCL model (BG_{SCL1}, 68.1%) are comparable to the baseline (BG, 67.6%). The adaptive perceptron HMM (BG_θ, 70.3%) improves by 2.7%, as much as model BG over B, again with a slightly larger variance. It is not clear why other methods do not improve as much. Speculatively, although we implemented several variants, SCL might benefit from further tuning as it involves several pre-processing steps. As for self training, the base tagger might be too inaccurate to support this technique. It is fair to assume that the additional hyperparameters available to our model, e.g., τ, provided some additional flexibility. We also experimented with a few variants of estimating θ on the development set; i.e., different splits of the unlabeled source/target data and different sampling modes: with and without replacement, number of trials. All of these aspects can have a significant impact on the quality of the model. This point brings up a more general issue with the type of approach explored here: while adapting the class priors seems easier than adapting the full model it is not trivial to encode noisy world knowledge into meaningful priors. Alternatively, in the presence of some labeled data one could optimize θ directly. This information could be also elicited from domain experts. Another interesting alternative is the unsupervised estimation via EM as in (Chan and Ng, 2006).

Overall, adaptation from BBN-4 to CoNLL is harder than from CoNLL to BBN-4. A possible explanation is that adapting from specific to general is harder then in the opposite direction: the specific corpus is more heavily biased towards a domain (finance). This intuition is compatible with the baselines performing better in the CoNLL to BBN-4 direction. However, the opposite argument, that adapting from specific to general should be easier, has some appeal as well; e.g., if more general means higher entropy it seems easier to make a distribution more uniform than finding the right peak.

In general, all adaptive techniques we evaluated provided only marginal improvements over the baseline (BG) model. To put things in context, it is useful to recall that when evaluated in domain the CoNLL and BBN-4 taggers (model BG) achieve, respectively, 92.7% and 91.6% average F-scores on the test data. As the results illustrate there is a considerable drop in out domain accuracy, significantly alleviated by adding features from gazetteers and to some extent by other methods. Following Dredze *et al.* (2007) we hypothesize that a significant fraction of the loss is due to labeling inconsistencies between datasets. Although we did our best to optimize the benchmark methods it is possible that even better results could be achieved with self-training and SCL. However we stress that different methods get at different aspects of the problem: self-training targets data sparseness, SCL methods aims at generating better shared input representations, while our approach focuses on generating output distribution more compatible with the target data. It seems reasonable to expect that better adaptation performance would result from composite approaches, aiming at both better machine learning and task-specific aspects for the named entity recognition problem.

8 Conclusion

We investigated the model adaptation problem for named entity recognition where the base model is a discriminatively trained HMM (Collins, 2002). We hypothesized that part of the loss incurred in using a pre-trained model out of domain is due to its built-in class priors which do not match the class distribution of the out of domain data. To test this hypothesis, and attempt a solution, we propose to explicitly correct the prediction of the model for a given label by taking into account a noisy estimate of the label frequency in the target data. We found encouraging results from preliminary experiments. It might thus be worth investigating more principled formulations of this type of method, in particular to eliminate some heuristic aspects, improve unsupervised estimations, and generalize to other classification tasks beyond NER.

Acknowledgments

We would like to thank the anonymous reviewers for useful comments and pointers to related work.

References

Rie Kubota Ando. 2004. Exploiting unannotated corpora for tagging and chunking. In *Proceedings of ACL 2004*. Association for Computational Linguistics.

BBN. 2005. Pronoun coreference and entity type corpus. *Linguistic Data Consortium (LDC) catalog number LDC2005T33*.

John Blitzer, Ryan McDonald, and Fernando Pereira. 2006. Domain adaptation with structural correspondence learning. In *Proceedings of EMNLP 2006*. Association for Computational Linguistics.

John Blitzer, Mark Dredzde, and Fernando Pereira. 2007. Biographies, bollywood, boom-boxes, and blenders: Domain adaptation for sentiment classification. In *Proceedings of ACL 2007*.

Yee Seng Chan and Hwee Tou Ng. 2006. Estimating class priors in domain adaptation for word sense disambiguation. In *Proceedings of Coling-ACL*, pages 89–96. Association for Computational Linguistics.

Eugene Charniak and Mark Johnson. 2005. Coarse-to-fine n-best parsing and MaxEnt discriminative reranking. In *Proceedings of ACL 2005*, pages 173–180. Association for Computational Linguistics.

Ciprian Chelba and Alex Acero. 2004. Adaptation of maximum entropy capitalizer: Little data can help a lot. In *Proceedings of EMNLP*, pages 285–292. Association for Computational Linguistics.

Massimiliano Ciaramita and Yasemin Altun. 2005. Named-entity recognition in novel domains with external lexical knowledge. In *Advances in Structured Learning for Text and Speech Processing (NIPS 2005)*.

Massimiliano Ciaramita and Yasemin Altun. 2006. Broad-coverage sense disambiguation and information extraction with a supersense sequence tagger. In *Proceedings of EMNLP*, pages 594–602. Association for Computational Linguistics.

Michael Collins. 2002. Discriminative training methods for hidden Markov models: Theory and experiments with perceptron algorithms. In *Proceedings of EMNLP 2002*, pages 1–8.

Hamish Cunningham, Diana Maynard, Kalina Bontcheva, and Valentin Tablan. 2002. GATE: A framework and graphical development environment for robust NLP tools and applications. In *Proceedings of ACL 2002*. Association for Computational Linguistics.

Hal Daumé III. 2007. Frustratingly easy domain adaptation. In *Proceedings of ACL*. Association for Computational Linguistics.

Mark Dredze, John Blitzer, Pratha Pratim Talukdar, Kuzman Ganchev, Joao Graca, and Fernando Pereira. 2007. Frustratingly hard domain adaptation for parsing. In *Proceedings of CoNLL Shared Task 2007*. Association for Computational Linguistics.

Y. Freund and R.E. Schapire. 1999. Large margin classification using the perceptron algorithm. *Machine Learning*, 37:277–296.

David McClosky, Eugene Charniak, and Mark Johnson. 2006. Reranking and self-training for parser adaptation. In *Proceedings of COLING-ACL 2006*, pages 337–344. Association for Computational Linguistics.

Peter Mika, Massimiliano Ciaramita, Hugo Zaragoza, and Jordi Atserias. 2008. Learning to tag and tagging to learn: A case study on Wikipedia. *IEEE Intelligent Systems*, 23(5):26–33.

Nam Nguyen and Yunsong Guo. 2007. Comparison of sequence labeling algorithms and extensions. In *Proceedings of ICML 2007*, pages 681–688.

Erik F. Tjong Kim Sang and Fien De Muelder. 2003. Introduction to the CoNLL-2003 shared task: Language-independent named entity recognition. In *Proceedings of CoNLL 2003 Shared Task*, pages 142–147. Association for Computational Linguistics.

Context Adaptation in Statistical Machine Translation Using Models with Exponentially Decaying Cache

Jörg Tiedemann
Department of Linguistics and Philology
Uppsala University, Uppsala/Sweden
jorg.tiedemann@lingfil.uu.se

Abstract

We report results from a domain adaptation task for statistical machine translation (SMT) using cache-based adaptive language and translation models. We apply an exponential decay factor and integrate the cache models in a standard phrase-based SMT decoder. Without the need for any domain-specific resources we obtain a 2.6% relative improvement on average in BLEU scores using our dynamic adaptation procedure.

1 Introduction

Most data-driven approaches to natural language processing (NLP) are subject to the well-known problem of lack of portability to new domains/genres. Usually there is a substantial drop in performance when testing on data from a domain different to the training data. Statistical machine translation is no exception. Despite its popularity, standard SMT approaches fail to provide a framework for general application across domains unless appropriate training data is available and used in parameter estimation and tuning.

The main problem is the general assumption of independent and identically distributed (i.i.d.) variables in machine learning approaches applied in the estimation of static global models. Recently, there has been quite some attention to the problem of domain switching in SMT (Zhao et al., 2004; Ueffing et al., 2007; Civera and Juan, 2007; Bertoldi and Federico, 2009) but ground breaking success is still missing. In this paper we report our findings in dynamic model adaptation using cache-based techniques when applying a standard model to the task of translating documents from a very different domain.

The remaining part of the paper is organized as follows: First, we will motivate the chosen approach by reviewing the general phenomenon of repetition and consistency in natural language text. Thereafter, we will briefly discuss the dynamic extensions to language and translation models applied in the experiments presented in the second last section followed by some final conclusions.

2 Motivation

Domain adaptation can be tackled in various ways. An obvious choice for empirical systems is to apply supervised techniques in case domain-specific training data is available. It has been shown that small(er) amounts of in-domain data are sufficient for such an approach (Koehn and Schroeder, 2007). However, this is not really a useful alternative for truly open-domain systems, which will be confronted with changing domains all the time including many new, previously unknown ones among them.

There are also some interesting approaches to dynamic domain adaptation mainly using flexible mixture models or techniques for the automatic selection of appropriate resources (Hildebrand et al., 2005; Foster and Kuhn, 2007; Finch and Sumita, 2008). Ideally, a system would adjust itself to the current context (and thus to the current domain) without the need of explicit topic mixtures. Therefore, we like to investigate techniques for general context adaptation and their use in out-of-domain translation.

There are two types of properties in natural language and translation that we like to explore. First of all, repetition is very common – much more than standard stochastic language models would predict. This is especially true for content words. See, for instance, the sample of a medical document shown in figure 1. Many content words are repeated in close context. Hence, appropriate language models should incorporate changing occurrence likelihoods to account for these very common repetitions. This is exactly what adaptive language models try to do (Bellegarda, 2004).

Proceedings of the 2010 Workshop on Domain Adaptation for Natural Language Processing, ACL 2010, pages 8–15,
Uppsala, Sweden, 15 July 2010.

"They may also have **episodes** of depression . Abilify is used to treat moderate to severe **manic episodes** and to prevent **manic episodes** in patients who have responded to the **medicine** in the past . The solution for injection is used for the rapid control of agitation or disturbed behaviour when taking the **medicine** by mouth is not appropriate . The **medicine** can only be obtained with a prescription ."

Figure 1: A short example from a document from the European Medicines Agency (EMEA)

Another known fact about natural language is consistency which is also often ignored in statistical models. A main problem in most NLP applications is ambiguity. However, ambiguity is largely removed within specific domains and contexts in which ambiguous items have a well-defined and consistent meaning. This effect of "meaning consistency" also known as the principle of "one sense per discourse" has been applied in word sense disambiguation with quite some success (Gale et al., 1992). For machine translation this means that adapting to the local domain and sticking to consistent translation choices within a discourse seems to be better than using a global static model and context independent translations of sentences in isolation. For an illustration, look at the examples in figure 2 taken from translated movie subtitles. Interesting is not only the consistent meaning of "honey" within each discourse but also the consistent choice among equivalent translations (synonyms "älskling" och "gumman"). Here, the distinction between "honey" and "sweetheart" has been transferred to Swedish using consistent translations.

The 10 commandments	**Kerd ma lui**
To some land flowing with milk and **honey**! Till ett land fullt av mjölk och **honung**. I've never tasted **honey**. Jag har aldrig smakat **honung**. ...	Mari **honey** ... Mari, **gumman** ... **Sweetheart**, where are you going? **Älskling**, var ska du? ... Who was that, **honey**? Vem var det, **gumman**?

Figure 2: Consistency in subtitle translations

In summary: Repetition and consistency are very important when modeling natural language and translation. A proper translation engine should move away from translating sentences in isolation but should consider wider context to include these discourse phenomena. In the next section we discuss the cache-based models that we implemented to address this challenge.

3 Cache-based Models

The main idea behind cache-based language models (Kuhn and Mori, 1990) is to mix a large global (static) language model with a small local (dynamic) model estimated from recent items in the history of the input stream. It is common to use simple linear interpolations and fixed cache sizes k (100-5000 words) to achieve this: $P(w_n|history) = (1-\lambda)P_{n-gram}(w_n|history) + \lambda P_{cache}(w_n|history)$

Due to data sparseness one is usually restricted to simple cache models. However, unigram models are often sufficient and smoothing is not necessary due to the interpolation with the smoothed background model. From the language modeling literature we know that caching is an efficient way to reduce perplexity (usually leading to modest improvements on in-domain data and large improvements on out-of-domain data). Table 1 shows this effect yielding 53% reduction of perplexity on our out-of-domain data.

	different settings for λ			
cache	0.05	0.1	0.2	0.3
0	376.1	376.1	376.1	376.1
50	270.7	259.2	*256.4*	264.9
100	261.1	246.6	*239.2*	243.3
500	252.2	233.1	219.1	*217.0*
1000	240.6	218.0	199.2	*192.9*
2000	234.6	209.6	187.9	*179.1*
5000	235.3	209.1	185.8	**175.8**
10000	237.6	210.7	186.6	*176.1*
20000	239.9	212.5	187.7	*176.7*

Table 1: Perplexity of medical texts (EMEA) using a language model estimated on Europarl and a unigram cache component

Even though a simple unigram cache is quite effective it now requires a careful optimization of its size. In order to avoid the dependence on cache size and to account for recency a decaying factor can be introduced (Clarkson and Robinson, 1997):

$$P_{cache}(w_n|w_{n-k}..w_{n-1}) \approx \frac{1}{Z}\sum_{i=n-k}^{n-1} I(w_n = w_i)e^{-\alpha(n-i)}$$

Here, $I(A) = 1$ if A is true and 0 otherwise. Z is a normalizing constant. Figure 3 illustrates the effect of cache decay on our data yielding another significant reduction in perplexity (even though

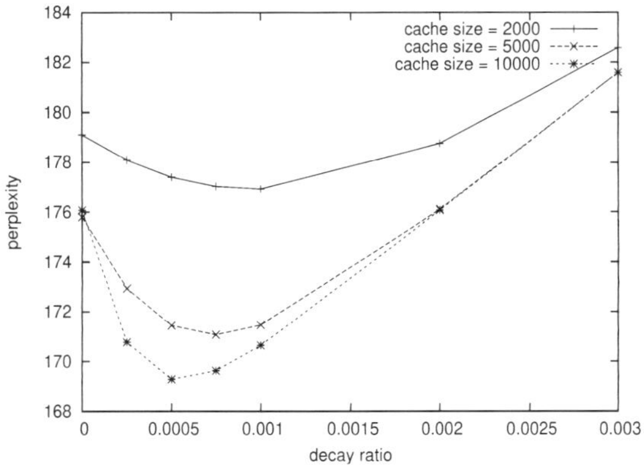

Figure 3: Out-of-domain perplexity using language models with decaying cache.

the improvement is much less impressive than the one obtained by introducing the cache).

The motivation of using these successful techniques in SMT is obvious. Language models play a crucial role in fluency ranking and a better fit to real data (supporting the tendency of repetition) should be preferred. This, of course, assumes correct translation decisions in the history in our SMT setting which will almost never be the case. Furthermore, simple cache models like the unigram model may wrongly push forward certain expressions without considering local context when using language models to discriminate between various translation candidates. Therefore, successfully applying these adaptive language models in SMT is surprisingly difficult (Raab, 2007) especially due to the risk of adding noise (leading to error propagation) and corrupting local dependencies.

In SMT another type of adaptation can be applied: cache-based adaptation of the translation model. Here, not only the repetition of content words is supported but also the consistency of translations as discussed earlier. This technique has already been tried in the context of interactive machine translation (Nepveu et al., 2004) in which cache features are introduced to adapt both the language model and the translation model. However, in their model they require an automatic alignment of words in the user edited translation and the source language input. In our experiments we investigate a close integration of the caching procedure into the decoding process of fully automatic translation. For this, we fill our cache with translation options used in the best (final) translation hypothesis of previous sentences. In our implementation of the translation model cache we use again a decaying factor in order to account for recency. For known source language items (f_n for which translation options exist in the cache) the following formula is used to compute the cache translation score:

$$\phi_{cache}(e_n|f_n) = \frac{\sum_{i=1}^{K} I(\langle e_n, f_n \rangle = \langle e_i, f_i \rangle) * e^{-\alpha i}}{\sum_{i=1}^{K} I(f_n = f_i)}$$

Unknown items receive a score of zero. This score is then used as an additional feature in the standard log-linear model of phrase-based SMT[1].

4 Experiments

Our experiments are focused on the unsupervised dynamic adaptation of language and translation models to a new domain using the cache-based mixture models as described above. We apply these techniques to a standard task of translating French to English using a model trained on the publicly available Europarl corpus (Koehn, 2005) using standard settings and tools such as the Moses toolkit (Koehn et al., 2007), GIZA++ (Och and Ney, 2003) and SRILM (Stolcke, 2002). The log-linear model is then tuned as usual with minimum error rate training (Och, 2003) on a separate development set coming from the same domain (Europarl). We modified SRILM to include a decaying cache model and implemented the phrase translation cache within the Moses decoder. Furthermore, we added the caching procedures and other features for testing the adaptive approach. Now we can simply switch the cache models on or off using additional command-line arguments when running Moses as usual.

4.1 Experimental Setup

For testing we chose to use documents from the medical domain coming from the EMEA corpus that is part of the freely available collection of parallel corpora OPUS[2] (Tiedemann, 2009). The reason for selecting this domain is that these documents include very consistent instructions and repetitive texts which ought to favor our caching techniques. Furthermore, they are very different

[1]Logarithmic values are used in the actual implementation which are floored to a low constant in case of zero ϕ scores.

[2]The OPUS corpus is available at this URL: `http://www.let.rug.nl/tiedeman/OPUS/`.

from the training data and, thus, domain adaptation is very important for proper translations. We randomly selected 102 pairs of documents with altogether 5,478 sentences. Sentences have an average length of about 19 tokens with a lot of variation among them. Documents are compiled from the European Public Assessment Reports (EPAR) which reflect scientific conclusions at the end of a centralized evaluation procedure for medical products. They include a lot of domain-specific terminology, short facts, lists and tables but also detailed textual descriptions of medicines and their use. The overall lowercased type/token ratio in the English part of our test collection is about 0.045 which indicates quite substantial repetitions in the text. This ratio is, however, much higher for individual documents.

In the experiment each document is processed individually in order to apply appropriate discourse breaks. The baseline score for applying a standard phrase-based SMT model yields an average score of 28.67 BLEU per document (28.60 per sentence) which is quite reasonable for an out-of-domain test. Intuitively, the baseline performance should be crucial for the adaptation. As discussed earlier the cache-based approach assumes correct history and better baseline performance should increase the chance of adding appropriate items to the cache.

4.2 Applying the LM Cache

In our first experiment we applied a decaying unigram cache in the language model. We performed a simple linear search on a separate development set for optimizing the interpolation weight which gave as a value of $\lambda = 0.001$. The size of the cache was set to 10,000 and the decay factor was set to $\alpha = 0.0005$ (according to our findings in figure 3). The results on our test data compared to the standard model are illustrated (with white boxes) in figure 4.

There is quite some variation in the effect of the cache LM on our test documents. The translations of most EMEA documents could be improved according to BLEU scores, some of them substantially, whereas others degraded slightly. Note that the documents differ in size and some of them are very short which makes it a bit difficult to interpret and directly compare these scores. On average the BLEU score is improved by 0.43 points per document and 0.39 points per sentence. This might

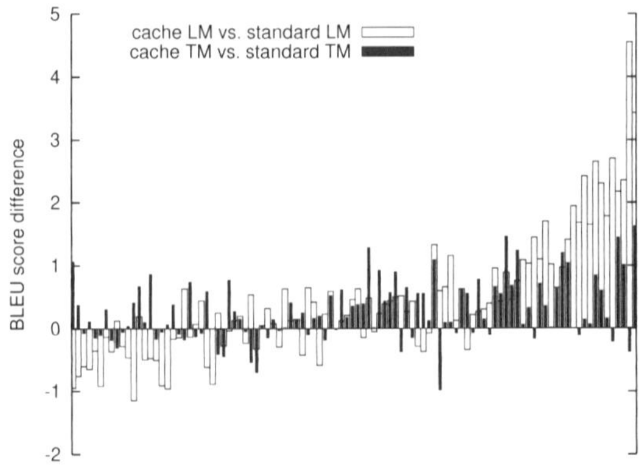

Figure 4: The differences in BLEU between a standard model and models with cache for 102 EMEA documents (sorted by overall BLEU score gain – see figure 5)

be not as impressive as we were hoping for after the tremendous perplexity reduction presented earlier. However, considering the simplicity of the approach that does not require any additional resources nor training it is still a valuable achievement.

4.3 Applying the TM Cache

In the next experiment we tested the effect of the TM cache on translation quality. Using our hypothesis of translation consistency we expected another gain on our test set. In order to reduce problems of noise we added two additional constraints: We only cache phrases that contain at least one word longer than 4 characters (a simplistic attempt to focus on content words rather than function words) and we only cache translation options for which the transition costs (of adding this option to the current hypothesis) in the global decoding model is larger than a given threshold (an attempt to use some notion of confidence for the current phrase pair; in our experiments we used a log score of -4). Using this setup and applying the phrase cache in decoding we obtained the results illustrated with filled boxes in the figure 4 above.

Again, we can observe a varied outcome but mostly improvements. The impact of the phrase translation cache (with a size of 5,000 items) is not as strong as for the language model cache which might be due to the rather conservative settings ($\lambda = 0.001$, $\alpha = 0.001$) and the fact that matching phrase pairs are less likely to appear than matching target words. On average the gain is about 0.275

BLEU points per document (0.26 per sentence).

4.4 Combining the Cache Models

Finally, we applied both types of cache in one common system using the same settings from the individual runs. The differences to the baseline model are shown in figure 5.

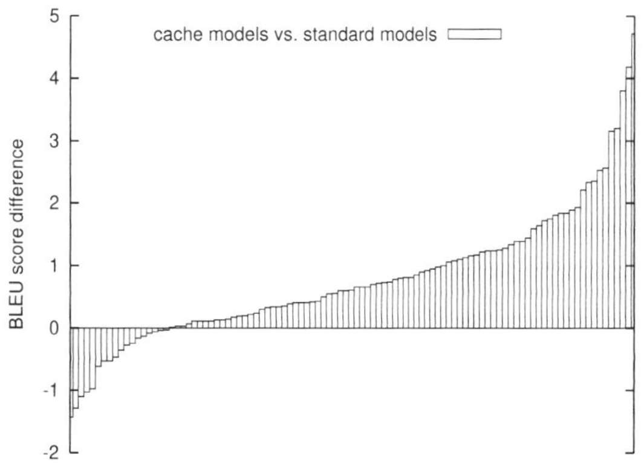

Figure 5: The BLEU score differences between a standard model and a model with cache for both TM and LM (sorted by BLEU score gain).

In most cases, applying the two types of cache together has a positive effect on the final BLEU score. Now, we see only a few documents with a drop in translation performance. On average the gain has increased to about 0.78 BLEU points per document (0.74 per sentence) which is about 2.7% relative improvement compared to the baseline (2.6% per sentence).

5 Discussion

Our experiments seem to suggest that caching could be a way to improve translation quality on a new domain. However, the differences are small and the assumption that previous translation hypotheses are good enough to be cached is risky. One obvious question is if the approach is robust enough to be helpful in general. If that is the the case we should also see positive effects on in-domain data where a cache model could adjust to topical shifts within that domain. In order to test this ability we ran an experiment with the 2006 test data from the workshop on statistical machine translation (Koehn and Monz, 2006) using the same models and settings as above. This resulted in the following scores (lowercased BLEU):

$BLEU_{baseline}$ = 32.46 (65.0/38.3/25.4/17.6, BP=0.999)
$BLEU_{cache}$ = 31.91 (65.1/38.1/25.1/17.3, BP=0.991)

Clearly, the cache models failed on this test even though the difference between the two runs is not large. There is a slight improvement in unigram matches (first value in brackets) but a drop on larger n-gram scores and also a stronger brevity penalty (BP). This could be an effect of the simplicity of the LM cache (a simple unigram model) which may improve the choice of individual lexical items but without respecting contextual dependencies.

One difference is that the in-domain data was translated in one step without clearing the cache at topical shifts. EMEA documents were translated one by one with empty caches at the beginning. It is now the question if proper initialization is essential and if there is a correlation between document length and the effect of caching. How much data is actually needed to take advantage of cached items and is there a point where a positive effect degrades because of topical shifts within the document? Let us, therefore, have a look at the relation between document length and BLEU score gain in our test collection (figure 6).

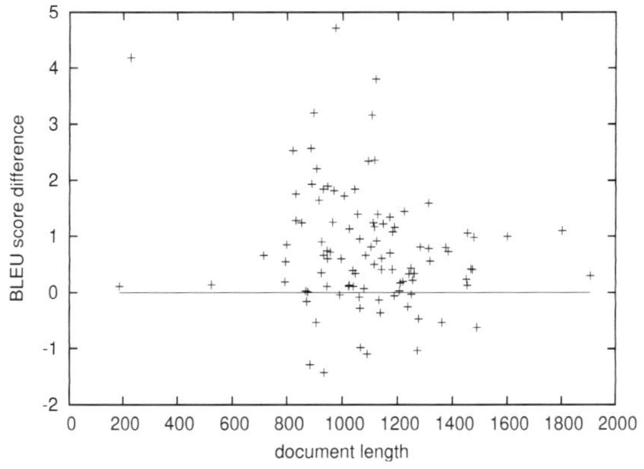

Figure 6: Correlation between document lengths (in number of tokens) and BLEU score gains with caching.

Concluding from this figure there does not seem to be any correlation. The length of the document does not seem to influence the outcome. What else could be the reason for the different behaviour among our test documents? One possibility is the quality of baseline translations assuming that better performance increases the chance of caching correct translation hypotheses. Figure 7 plots the BLEU score gains in comparison with the baseline scores.

Again, no immediate correlation can be seen.

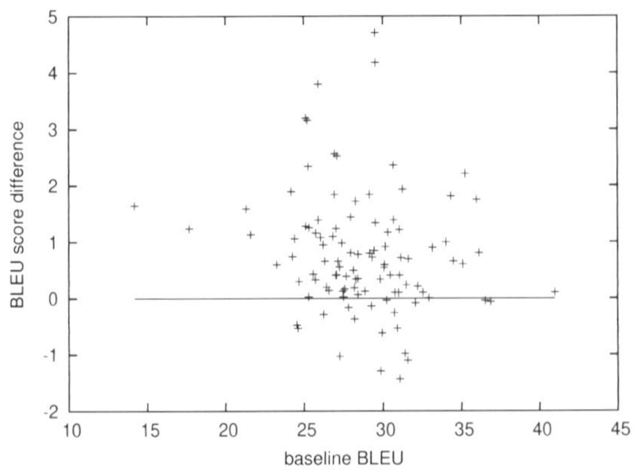

Figure 7: Correlation between baseline BLEU scores and BLEU score gains with caching

The baseline performance does not seem to give any clues for a possible success of caching. This comes as a surprise as our intuitions suggested that good baseline performance should be essential for the adaptive approach.

Another reason for their success should be the amount of repetition (especially among content words) in the documents to be translated. An indication for this can be given by type/token ratios assuming that documents with lower ratios contain a larger amount of repetitive text. Figure 8 plots the type/token ratios of all test documents in comparison with the BLEU score gains obtained with caching.

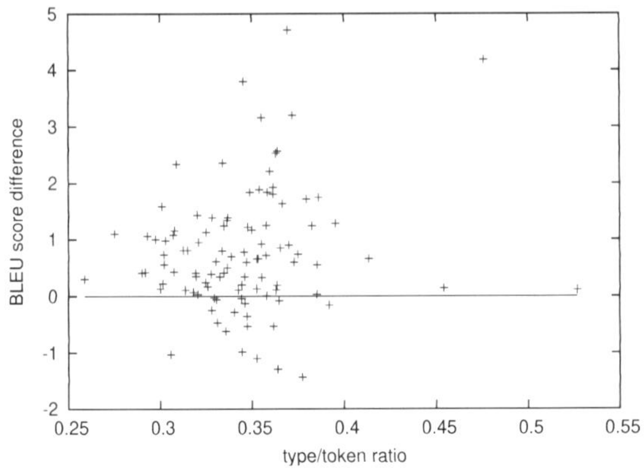

Figure 8: Correlation between type/token ratios and BLEU score gains with caching

Once again there does not seem to be any obvious correlation. So far we could not identify any particular property of documents that might help to reliably predict the success of caching. The answer is probably a combination of various factors. Further experiments are needed to see the effect on different data sets and document types.

Note that some results may also be an artifact of the automatic evaluation metrics applied. Qualitative evaluations using manual inspection could probably reveal important aspects of the caching approach. However, tracing changes caused by caching is rather difficult due to the interaction with other factors in the global decoding process. Some typical cases may still be identified. Figure 9 shows an example of a translation that has been improved in the cached model by making the translation more consistent (this is from a document that actually got a lower BLEU score in the end with caching).

baseline: report (evaluation of european public epar)
vivanza
in the short epar public
this document is a summary of the european public to evaluation report (epar) .

cache: report european public assessment (epar)
vivanza
epar to sum up the public
this document is a summary of the european public assessment report (epar) .

reference: european public assessment report (epar)
vivanza
epar summary for the public
this document is a summary of the european public assessment report (epar) .

Figure 9: A translation improved by caching.

Other improvements may not be recognized by automatic evaluation metrics and certain acceptable differences may be penalized. Look, for instance, at the examples in figure 10.

This is, of course, not a general claim that cache-based translations are more effected by this problem than, for example, the baseline system. However, this could be a direction for further investigations to quantify these issues.

6 Conclusions

In this paper we presented adaptive language and translation models that use an exponentially decaying cache. We applied these models to a domain adaptation task translating medical documents with a standard model trained on Europarl. On average the dynamic adaptation approach led to a gain of about 2.6% relative BLEU points per sentence. The main advantage of this approach is that it does not require any domain-specific train-

baseline:	the medication is issued on orders .
cache:	the medication is issued on **prescription-only** .
reference:	the medicine can **only** be obtained with a **prescription** .
baseline:	benefix **is a powder** keg , and a solvent to dissolve the injection for .
cache:	benefix **consists of a powder** and a solvent to dissolve the injection for .
reference:	benefix **is a powder** and solvent that are mixed together for injection .
baseline:	the principle of active benefix is the nonacog alfa (ix coagulation factor of recombinant) which favours the coagulation blood .
cache:	the principle of benefix is the nonacog alfa (ix coagulation factor of recombinant) which favours the coagulation blood .
reference:	benefix contains the active ingredient nonacog alfa (recombinant coagulation factor ix , which helps blood to clot) .
baseline:	**in any case** , it is benefix used ?
cache:	**in which case** it is benefix used ?
reference:	**what is** benefix used for ?
baseline:	benefix is used for the treatment and prevention of saignements among **patients with haemophilia b** (a disorder hémorragique hereditary due to a deficiency in factor ix) .
cache:	benefix is used for the treatment and prevention of saignements among **patients suffering haemophilia b** (a disorder hémorragique hereditary due to a lack factor in ix) .
reference:	benefix is used for the treatment and prevention of bleeding in **patients with haemophilia b** (an inherited bleeding disorder caused by lack of factor ix) .
baseline:	benefix can be used for adults and children **over** 6 years .
cache:	benefix can be used for adults and children **of more than** 6 years
reference:	benfix can be used in adults and children **over the age of** 6.

Figure 10: Examples translations with and without caching.

ing, tuning (assuming that interpolation weights and other cache parameters can be fixed after some initial experiments) nor the incorporation of any other in-domain resources. Cache based adaptation can directly be applied to any new domain and similar gains should be possible. However, a general conclusion cannot be drawn from our initial results presented in this paper. Further experiments are required to verify these findings and to explore the potentials of cache-based techniques. The main obstacle is the invalid assumption that initial translations are correct. The success of the entire method crucially depends on this assumption. Error propagation and the reinforcement of wrong decisions is the largest risk. Therefore, strategies to reduce noise in the cache are important and can still be improved using better selection criteria. A possible strategy could be to identify simple cases in a first run that can be used to reliably fill the cache and to use the full cache model on the entire text in a second run. Another idea for improvement is to attach weights to cache entries according to the translation costs assigned by the model. These weights could easily be incorporated into the cache scores returned for matching items. In future, we would like to explore these ideas and also possibilities to combine cache models with other types of adaptation techniques.

References

Jerome R. Bellegarda. 2004. Statistical language model adaptation: review and perspectives. *Speech Communication*, 42:93–108.

Nicola Bertoldi and Marcello Federico. 2009. Domain adaptation for statistical machine translation with monolingual resources. In *StatMT '09: Proceedings of the Fourth Workshop on Statistical Machine Translation*, pages 182–189, Morristown, NJ, USA. Association for Computational Linguistics.

Jorge Civera and Alfons Juan. 2007. Domain adaptation in statistical machine translation with mixture modelling. In *Proceedings of the Second Workshop on Statistical Machine Translation*, pages 177–180, Prague, Czech Republic. Association for Computational Linguistics.

P.R. Clarkson and A. J. Robinson. 1997. Language model adaptation using mixtures and an exponentially decaying cache. In *International Conference on Acoustics, Speech, and Signal Processing (ICASSP)*, pages 799–802, Munich, Germany.

Andrew Finch and Eiichiro Sumita. 2008. Dynamic model interpolation for statistical machine translation. In *StatMT '08: Proceedings of the Third Workshop on Statistical Machine Translation*, pages 208–215, Morristown, NJ, USA. Association for Computational Linguistics.

George Foster and Roland Kuhn. 2007. Mixture-model adaptation for SMT. In *Proceedings of the Second Workshop on Statistical Machine Translation*, pages 128–135, Prague, Czech Republic. Association for Computational Linguistics.

William A. Gale, Kenneth W. Church, and David Yarowsky. 1992. One sense per discourse. In *HLT '91: Proceedings of the workshop on Speech and Natural Language*, pages 233–237, Morristown, NJ, USA. Association for Computational Linguistics.

Almut Silja Hildebrand, Matthias Eck, Stephan Vogel, and Alex Waibel. 2005. Adaptation of the translation model for statistical machine translation based on information retrieval. In *Proceedings of the 10th Conference of the European Association for Machine Translation (EAMT)*, pages 133–142, Budapest.

Philipp Koehn and Christof Monz, editors. 2006. *Proceedings on the Workshop on Statistical Machine Translation*. Association for Computational Linguistics, New York City, June.

Philipp Koehn and Josh Schroeder. 2007. Experiments in domain adaptation for statistical machine translation. In *Proceedings of the Second Workshop on Statistical Machine Translation*, pages 224–227, Prague, Czech Republic. Association for Computational Linguistics.

Philipp Koehn, Hieu Hoang, Alexandra Birch, Chris Callison-Burch, Marcello Federico, Nicola Bertoldi, Brooke Cowan, Wade Shen, Christine Moran, Richard Zens, Chris Dyer, Ondřej Bojar, Alexandra Constantin, and Evan Herbst. 2007. Moses: open source toolkit for statistical machine translation. In *ACL '07: Proceedings of the 45th Annual Meeting of the ACL on Interactive Poster and Demonstration Sessions*, pages 177–180, Morristown, NJ, USA. Association for Computational Linguistics.

Philipp Koehn. 2005. Europarl: A parallel corpus for statistical machine translation. In *Proceedings of the 10th Machine Translation Summit (MT Summit X)*.

Roland Kuhn and Renato De Mori. 1990. A cache-based natural language model for speech recognition. *IEEE Transactions on Pattern Analysis and Machine Intelligence*, 12(6):570–583.

Laurent Nepveu, Lapalme, Guy, Langlais, Philippe, and George Foster. 2004. Adaptive Language and Translation Models for Interactive Machine Translation. In *Proceedings of the 9th Conference on Empirical Methods in Natural Language Processing (EMNLP)*, pages 190–197, Barcelona, Spain.

Franz Josef Och and Hermann Ney. 2003. A systematic comparison of various statistical alignment models. *Computational Linguistics*, 29(1):19–51.

Franz Josef Och. 2003. Minimum error rate training in statistical machine translation. In *ACL '03: Proceedings of the 41st Annual Meeting on Association for Computational Linguistics*, pages 160–167, Morristown, NJ, USA. Association for Computational Linguistics.

Martin Raab. 2007. *Language Modeling for Machine Translation*. VDM Verlag, Saarbrücken, Germany.

Andreas Stolcke. 2002. SRILM - an extensible language modeling toolkit. In *Proceedings of the 7th international conference on spoken language processing (ICSLP 2002)*, pages 901–904, Denver, CO, USA.

Jörg Tiedemann. 2009. News from OPUS - A collection of multilingual parallel corpora with tools and interfaces. In *Recent Advances in Natural Language Processing*, volume V, pages 237–248. John Benjamins, Amsterdam/Philadelphia.

Nicola Ueffing, Gholamreza Haffari, and Anoop Sarkar. 2007. Semi-supervised model adaptation for statistical machine translation. *Machine Translation*, 21(2):77–94.

Bing Zhao, Matthias Eck, and Stephan Vogel. 2004. Language model adaptation for statistical machine translation with structured query models. In *COLING '04: Proceedings of the 20th international conference on Computational Linguistics*, page 411, Morristown, NJ, USA. Association for Computational Linguistics.

Domain Adaptation to Summarize Human Conversations

Oana Sandu, Giuseppe Carenini, Gabriel Murray, and Raymond Ng
University of British Columbia
Vancouver, Canada
{oanas,carenini,gabrielm,rng}@cs.ubc.ca

Abstract

We are interested in improving the summarization of conversations by using domain adaptation. Since very few email corpora have been annotated for summarization purposes, we attempt to leverage the labeled data available in the multi-party meetings domain for the summarization of email threads. In this paper, we compare several approaches to supervised domain adaptation using out-of-domain labeled data, and also try to use unlabeled data in the target domain through semi-supervised domain adaptation. From the results of our experiments, we conclude that with some in-domain labeled data, training in-domain with no adaptation is most effective, but that when there is no labeled in-domain data, domain adaptation algorithms such as structural correspondence learning can improve summarization.

1 Introduction

On a given day, many people engage in conversations via several modalities, including face-to-face speech, telephone, email, SMS, chat, and blogs. Being able to produce automatic summaries of multi-party conversations occurring in one or several of these modalities would enable the parties involved to keep track of and make sense of this diverse data. However, summarizing spoken dialogue is more challenging than summarizing written monologues such as books and articles, as speech tends to be more fragmented and disfluent.

We are interested in using both fully and semi-supervised techniques to produce extractive summaries for conversations, where each sentence of a text is labeled with its informativeness, and a subset of sentences are concatenated into an extractive summary of the text. In previous work (Murray and Carenini, 2008), it has been shown that conversations in different modalities can be effectively characterized by a set of "conversational" features that are useful in detecting informativeness for the task of extractive summarization. However, because of privacy concerns, annotated corpora are rarely publicly available for conversational data, including for the email domain. One promising solution to this problem is domain adaptation, which aims to use labeled data in a well-studied source domain and a limited amount of labeled data from a different target domain to train a model that performs well in that target domain. In this work, we investigate using domain adaptation that leverages labeled data in the domain of meetings along with labeled and unlabeled email data for summarizing email threads. We evaluate several domain adaptation algorithms, using both a small set of conversational features and a large set of simple lexical features to determine what settings will yield the best results for summarizing email conversations. In our experiments, we do not get a significant improvement from using out-of-domain data in addition to in-domain data in supervised domain adaptation, though in the setting where only unlabeled in-domain data is available, we gain from using it through structural correspondence learning. We also observe that conversational features are more useful in supervised methods, whereas lexical features are better leveraged in semi-supervised adaptation.

The next section surveys past research in domain adaptation and in summarizing conversational data. In section 3 we present the corpora and feature sets we used, and we describe our experimental setting in section 4. We then compare the performance of different methods in section 5 and draw conclusions in section 6.

Proceedings of the 2010 Workshop on Domain Adaptation for Natural Language Processing, ACL 2010, pages 16–22,
Uppsala, Sweden, 15 July 2010.

2 Related Work

We give an overview first of work on supervised and semi-supervised domain adaptation, then of research on summarization of conversations.

2.1 Supervised Domain Adaptation

Many domain adaptation methods have been proposed for the supervised case, where a small amount of labeled data in the target domain is used along with a larger amount of labeled source data. Two baseline approaches are to train only on the source data or only on target training data. One way of using information from both domains is merging the source and target labeled data sets and training a model on the combination. A method inspired by boosting is to take a linear combination of the predictions of two classifiers, one trained on the source and one trained on the target training data. Another simple method is to train a predictor on the source data, run it on the target data, and then use its predictions on each instance as additional features for a target-trained model. This was first introduced by Florian et al. (2004), who applied it to multilingual named entity recognition.

The prior method of domain adaptation by Chelba and Acero (2006) involves using the source data to find optimal parameter values of a maximum entropy model on that data, and then setting these as a prior on the values of a model trained on the target data. They find improvement in a capitalizer that adapts using out-of-domain and a small amount of in-domain data versus only training on out-of-domain WSJ data. Similar to the prior method, Daume's MEGA model also trains a MEMM. It achieves domain adaptation through hyperparameters that indicate whether an instance is generated by a source, target, or general distribution, and finds the optimal values of the parameters through conditional EM (Daume and Marcu, 2006). A simpler method of domain adaptation, that achieves a performance similar to prior and MEGA, was proposed by Daume (2007) and successfully applied to a variety of NPL sequence labeling problems, such as named entity recognition, shallow parsing, and part-of-speech (POS) tagging. Furthermore, this approach is straightforward to apply by copying feature values so there is a source version, a target version, and a general version of the feature, and was found to be faster to train than MEGA and prior. For all these reasons, we use Daume's method and not the other two in our experiments.

2.2 Semi-supervised Domain Adaptation

Because unlabeled data is usually much easier to collect than labeled data in a new domain, semi-supervised domain adaptation methods that exploit unlabeled data are potentially very useful.

In self-training, a training set is used that is originally composed of labeled data, and repeatedly augmented with the highest confidence predictions on unlabeled data. McClosky et al. (2006) apply this in a domain adaptation setting for parsing: with only unlabeled data in the target Brown domain, and labeled and unlabeled datasets in the news domain (WSJ and NANC respectively), a self-trained reranking parser performs almost as well as a parser trained only on Brown labeled data. However, McClosky concludes that self-training alone is not beneficial, and most of the improvements they get over previous work on domain adaptation for parsing are due to using the reranker to select the candidate instances produced in each iteration of self-training. Thus, one of the issues addressed in this paper is to asses whether self-training is useful for domain adaptation.

A more sophisticated semi-supervised domain adaptation method is structural correspondence learning (SCL). SCL uses unlabeled data to determine correspondences between features in the two domains by correlating them with so-called pivot features, which are features exhibiting similar behaviors in the source and target domains. Blitzer applied this algorithm successfully to POS tagging (Blitzer et al., 2006) and sentiment classification (Blitzer et al., 2007). SCL seems promising for other tasks as well, for example parse disambiguation (Plank, 2009).

2.3 Summarization

We would like to use domain adaptation to aid in summarizing multi-party conversations hailing from different modalities. This contrasts with much of previous work on summarization of conversations, which has focused on domain-specific features (e.g., Rambow et al, 2004). We will treat summarization as a supervised binary classification problem where the sentences of a conversation are rated by their informativeness and a subset is selected to form an extractive summary. Research in meeting summarization relevant to our task has investigated the utility of employing a large feature set including prosodic information, speaker status, lexical and structural discourse features (Murray et al., 2006; Galley, 2006). For email summarization, we view an email thread as a conversation. For summarizing email threads, Rambow (2004) used lexical features such as tf.idf, features that considered the thread to be a sequence of turns, and email-specific features such as number of recipients and the subject line. Asynchronous multi-party conversations were successfully represented for summarization through a small number of conversational features by Murray and Carenini (2008). This paved the way to cross-domain conversation summarization by representing both email threads and meetings with a set of common conversational features. The work we present here investigates using data from both emails and meetings in summarizing emails, and compares using conversational versus lexical features.

3 Summarization setting

Because the meetings domain has a large corpus, AMI, annotated for summarization, we will use it as the source domain for adaptation and the email domain as the target, with data from the Enron corpus as unlabeled email data, and the BC3 corpus as test data.

3.1 Datasets

The AMI meeting corpus: We use the *scenario* portion of the AMI corpus (Carletta et al., 2005), for which groups of four participants take part in a series of four meetings and play roles within a fictitious company. While the scenario given to them is artificial, the speech and the actions are completely spontaneous and natural. The dataset contains approximately 115000 dialogue act (DA) segments. For the annotation, annotators wrote abstract summaries of each meeting and extracted transcript DA segments that best conveyed or supported the information in the abstracts. A many-to-many mapping between transcript DAs and sentences from the human abstract was obtained for each annotator, with three annotators assigned to each meeting. We consider a dialogue act to be a positive example if it is linked to a given human summary, and a negative example otherwise. Approximately 13% of the total DAs are ultimately labeled as positive.

The BC3 email corpus[1]**:** composed of 40 email threads from the World Wide Web Consortium (W3C) mailing list which feature a variety of topics such as web accessibility and planning face-to-face meetings. Each thread is annotated similarly to the AMI corpus, with three annotators authoring abstracts and linking email thread sentences to the abstract sentences.

The Enron email corpus[2]**:** a collection of emails released as part of the investigation into the Enron corporation, it has become a popular corpus for NLP research due to being realistic, naturally-occurring data from a corporate environment. We use 39 threads from this corpus to supplement the BC3 email data.

3.2 Features Used

We consider two sets of features for each sentence: a small set of conversational structure features, and a large set of lexical features.

Conversational features: We extract 24 conversational features from both the email and meetings domain, and which consider both emails and meetings to be conversations comprised of turns between multiple participants. For an email thread, a turn consists of a single email fragment in the exchange. Similarly, for meetings, a turn is a sequence of dialogue acts by the same speaker. The conversational features, which are described in detail in (Murray and Carenini, 2008), include sentence length, sentence position in the conversation and in the current turn, pause-style features, lexical cohesion, centroid scores, and features that measure how terms cluster between conversation participants and conversation turns.

Lexical features: We derive an extensive set of lexical features, originally proposed in (Murray et al., 2010) from the AMI and BC3 datasets, and then compute their occurrence in the Enron corpus. After throwing out features that occur less than five times, we end up with approximately 200,000 features. The features derived are: character trigrams, word bigrams, POS tag bigrams, word pairs, POS pairs, and varying instantiation ngram (VIN) features. For word pairs, we extract the ordered pairs of words that occur in the same sentence, and similarly for POS pairs. To derive VIN features, we take each word bigram w_1,w_2 and further represent it as two patterns p_1,w_2 and w_1,p_2 each consisting of a word and a POS tag.

3.3 Classifier

In all of our experiments, we train logistic regression classifiers using the *liblinear* toolkit[3]. This choice was partly motivated by our earlier summarization research, where logistic regression classifiers were compared alongside support

[1] http://www.cs.ubc.ca/labs/lci/bc3.html

[2] http://www.cs.cmu.edu/~enron/

[3] http://www.csie.ntu.edu.tw/~cjlin/liblinear/

vector machines. The two types of classifier yielded very similar results, with logistic regression classifiers being much faster to train.

3.4 Evaluation Metric

Given the predicted labels on a test set and the existing gold-standard labels of the test set data, in each of our experiments we compute the area under the receiver operator curve as a measure of performance. The area under the ROC (auROC) is a common summary statistic used to measure the quality of binary classification, where a perfect classifier would achieve an auROC of 1.0, and a random classifier, near 0.5.

4 Experiments

4.1 Experimental Design

The available labeled BC3 data totals about 3000 sentences, and the available labeled AMI data totals over 100,000 sentences, so for both efficiency and to not overwhelm the in-domain data, in each of our runs we subsample 10,000 sentences from the AMI data to use for training. After some initial experiments, where increasing the amount of target data beyond this did not improve accuracy, we decided not to incur the runtime cost of training on larger amounts of source data. Similarly, given that we extracted about 200,000 lexical features from our corpora, from our initial experiments trading off auROC and runtime, we decided to select a subset of 10,000 lexical features chosen by having the top mutual information with respect to the summarization labels. We did 5-fold cross-validation to split the target set into training and testing portions, and ran all the domain adaptation methods using the same split. We report the auROC performance of each method averaged over three runs of the 5-fold cross-validation. To test for significant differences between the performances of the various methods, we compute pairwise t-tests between the auROC values obtained on the same run. To account for an increased chance of false positives in reporting results of several pairwise t-tests, we report significance for p-values < 0.005 rather than at the customary 0.05 level.

4.2 Methods Implemented

We compare supervised domain adaptation methods to the baseline INDOMAIN, in which only the training folds of the target data are used for training. In the MERGE method, we simply combine the labeled source and target sets and train on their combination. For ENSEMBLE, we train a classifier on the source training data, a classifier on the target training data, run each of them on the target test data, and for each test instance compute the average of the two probabilities predicted by the classifiers and use it to make a label prediction. We could vary the trade-off between the contribution of the source and target classifier in ENSEMBLE and determine the optimal parameter by cross-validation, though for simplicity we used 0.5 which produced satisfying results. For the PRED approach, we use the source data to train a classifier, use it to make a prediction for the label of each point in the target data, and add the predicted probability as an additional feature to an in-domain trained classifier. The final supervised method FEAT-COPY (Daume, 2007) takes the existing features and extends the feature space by making a general, a source-specific, and a target-specific version of each feature. Hence, a sentence with features (x) gets represented as (x, x, 0) if it comes from the source domain, and as (x, 0, x) if it comes from the target domain.

For semi-supervised domain adaptation methods, our baseline does not exploit any unlabeled target data. We train a classifier on the source data only, and call this TRANSFER. In contrast our two semi-supervised methods try to leverage unlabeled target data to help a classifier trained with labeled source data be more suited to the target domain.

For the SCL approach, we implemented Blitzer's structural correspondence learning (SCL) algorithm. An important part of the algorithm is training a classifier for each of a set of m selected pivot features to determine the correlations of the other features with respect to the pivot. The m models' weights are combined in a matrix, and its SVD with truncation factor of k is then applied to the data to yield k new features for the data, that are added to the existing features. For the larger set of lexical features, we ran SCL with Blitzer's original choice of m=1000 and k=50, but since the computation was extremely time consuming we scale down m to 100. For the tests with conversational features, since the number of features is 24, we picked m=24 and k=24. We also test SCLSMALL, which uses the same algorithm as SCL to find augmented features, except it then uses only these k features to train, not adding them to the original features. This possibility was suggested in (Blitzer 2008).

As a second semi-supervised method, we implemented SELFTRAIN. The standard self-training algorithm we implemented, inspired by

Blum and Mitchell (1998), is to start with a labeled training set T, create a subset of a fixed size of the unlabeled data U, and then iterate training a classifier on T, making a prediction on the data in U, and take the highest-confidence positive p predictions and highest-confidence negative n predictions from U with their predicted labels to add to T before replenishing U from the rest of the unlabeled data. We picked the size of the subset U as 200, and to select the top p=3 and bottom n=17 predictions at each step in order to achieve a ratio of summary to total sentences of 15%, which is near to the known ratio of the labels for AMI.

method	indomain	merge	ensemble	featcopy	pred	transfer	selftrain	scl	sclsmall
using conversational features									
auROC	0.838	0.747	0.751	0.839	0.838	0.677	0.678	0.663	0.646
time(s)	0.79	2.42	2.64	8.44	5.38	2.08	100.2	52.85	66.74
using lexical features									
auROC	0.623	0.638	0.667	0.615	0.625	0.636	0.636	0.651	0.742
time(s)	4.87	13.64	13.77	78.63	30.99	9.73	448.8	813.7	828.3

Table 1. Performance and time of domain adaptation methods with the two feature sets

5 Results

In our first experiment, we ran all the domain adaptation methods on the data with conversational features; in our second experiment, we did the same on the data with lexical features. We computed the average of the auROCs and running times obtained for each method in each experiment. Table 1 lists the results of the supervised methods MERGE, ENSEMBLE, and FEATCOPY with baseline INDOMAIN, and the semi-supervised methods SELFTRAIN, SCL, and SCLSMALL with baseline TRANSFER.

The best results for supervised methods (and overall) are achieved by FEATCOPY, PRED, and INDOMAIN with the conversational features, with a similar performance that is significantly better than for MERGE and ENSEMBLE. However, for lexical features MERGE and ENSEMBLE beat their performance, with the significant differences from the baseline INDOMAIN being those of ENSEMBLE and FEATCOPY, the latter now being the worst performer.

For the set of lexical features, all semi-supervised methods improve on TRANSFER. In this setting, all of the differences are significant, with SCLSMALL generating a considerable gain of 10%. For the set of conversational features, SELFTRAIN yields an auROC similar to TRANSFER, and the small difference between the two is not significant. Unlike when using lexical features, SCL and SCLSMALL perform significantly worse than TRANSFER, though this is not unexpected. Because it relies on determining correlation between features, we believe that structural correspondence learning is more appropriate in a high rather than low-dimensional feature space.

Figure 1 shows, for each of the methods, a dark grey bar representing the auROC obtained with the set of conversational features next to a lighter grey one for the lexical features. For the supervised methods on the left (INDOMAIN to PRED), the conversational features yield better performance, and this by an absolute ROC difference of more than 5%. However, notice that no method outperform the baseline INDOMAIN. For the semi-supervised methods on the right, the difference in performance between the two feature sets is less marked, although the auROC of SCLSMALL with lexical features is exceptionally larger.

As shown in Table 1, every one of the domain adaptation methods has a higher average time with lexical features than with conversational features. The semi-supervised methods take longer than the fully supervised methods, and this is due to their algorithms involving more steps. Both SCL and SELFTRAIN take minutes instead of seconds to make a prediction, though their running times are more reasonable than with the initial parameter settings we used in preliminary experiments.

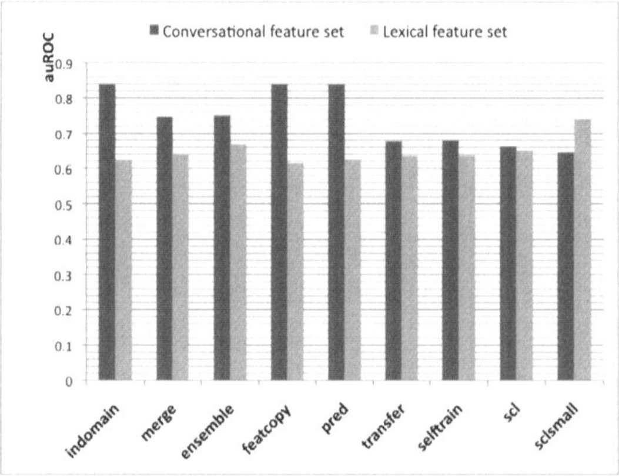

Figure 1. Comparison of auROCs of all domain adaptation methods and baselines

6 Conclusions and Future Work

This paper is a comparative study of the performance of several domain adaptation methods on the task of summarizing conversational data when a large amount of annotated data is available in the domain of meetings and a smaller (or no) amount of annotation exists in the target domain of email threads.

One surprising finding of our experiments is that of the methods we implemented, the best performance is achieved by training on in-domain data using conversational features. Hence, it seems that when sufficient labeled in-domain data is available, supervised domain adaptation is not useful for summarization of emails with the features and amounts of labeled data we used.

However, semi-supervised methods using unlabeled data and labeled out-of-domain data are useful in the absence of these labels, with the SCLSMALL method greatly outperforming the baseline. This is a promising result for using annotated corpora in well-studied domains or conversational modalities to summarize data in new domains.

In our experiments, we have explored the effectiveness of conversational and lexical features separately. The two sets of features differ in their impact on domain adaptation: with conversational features, no method improves significantly over the baseline, whereas with lexical features, the semi-supervised methods given no labeled target data perform better than the supervised baseline of training in-domain. One hypothesis to explain this is that lexical features behave similarly in the two domains, so training on the larger amount of labeled target data is beneficial, while conversational features are more domain specific, likely because emails and meetings are structured differently. As the next step in our work, we intend to combine the two sets of features. In doing this, we will have to ensure that the conversational features are not washed out by a very large number of lexical features.

A scenario of practical interest in domain adaptation for new domains is when the target domain has a considerable amount of unlabeled data and a subset of this data can easily be annotated by hand, for example five threads in the email domain. We are currently exploring injecting a small amount of labeled target data into the semi-supervised methods we have implemented to account for differences that cannot be observed in the unlabeled data. Blitzer (2008) did such an adjustment to SCL using a small amount of labeled target data to correct misaligned features and thus improve accuracy.

Finally, it may be worth investigating how to combine several of the methods, for example by adding the feature of PRED based on training a classifier on the source, alongside augmented features using more unlabeled data through SCL, and adding the highest-confidence labels from SELFTRAIN to the training set.

References

Blitzer, J. (2008). Domain Adaptation of Natural Language Processing Systems. PhD Thesis.

Blitzer, J., Dredze, M., & Pereira, F. (2007). Biographies, Bollywood, Boom-boxes and Blenders: Domain Adaptation for Sentiment Classification. In *Proc. of ACL 2007*.

Blitzer, J., McDonald, R., & Pereira, F. (2006). Domain adaptation with structural correspondence learning. In *Proc. of EMNLP 2006*.

Blum, A., & Mitchell, T. (1998). Combining labeled and unlabeled data with co-training. In *Proc. CLT*.

Carletta, J., Ashby, S., Bourban, S., Flynn, M., Guillemot, M. et al. (2005). The AMI meeting corpus: A pre-announcement. In *Proc. of MLMI 2005*.

Chelba, C., & Acero, A. (2006). Adaptation of maximum entropy capitalizer: Little data can help a lot. *Computer Speech & Language*, *20*(4), 382-399.

Daume III, H. (2007). Frustratingly easy domain adaptation. In *Proc. of ACL 2007*.

Daume III, H., & Marcu, D. (2006). Domain Adaptation for Statistical Classifiers. *Journal of Artificial Intelligence Research*, *26*, 101–126.

Florian, R., Hassan, H., Ittycheriah, A., Jing, H., Kambhatla, N., Luo, X., et al. (2004). A statistical model for multilingual entity detection and tracking. In *Proc. HLT-NAACL 2004*.

Galley, M. (2006). A skip-chain conditional random field for ranking meeting utterances by importance. In *Proc. of EMNLP 2006*.

McClosky, D., Charniak, E., & Johnson, M. (2006). Effective self-training for parsing. In *Proc. of HLT-NAACL 2006* .

Murray, G., & Carenini, G. (2008). Summarizing spoken and written conversations. In *Proc. of EMNLP 2008*.

Murray, G., Carenini, G., & Ng, R. (2010). Interpretation and transformation for abstracting conversations. In *Proc. of HLT-NAACL 2010*.

Murray, G., Renals, S., Moore, J., & Carletta, J. (2006). Incorporating speaker and discourse features into speech summarization. In *Proc. of HLT-NAACL 2006*.

Plank, B. (2009). Structural correspondence learning for parse disambiguation. In *Proc. of EACL 2009: Student Research Workshop*.

Rambow, O., Shrestha, L., & Chen, J. (2004). Summarizing email threads. In *Proc. of HLT-NAACL 2004*.

Exploring Representation-Learning Approaches to Domain Adaptation

Fei Huang and **Alexander Yates**
Temple University
Computer and Information Sciences
324 Wachman Hall
Philadelphia, PA 19122
{fei.huang,yates}@temple.edu

Abstract

Most supervised language processing systems show a significant drop-off in performance when they are tested on text that comes from a domain significantly different from the domain of the training data. Sequence labeling systems like part-of-speech taggers are typically trained on newswire text, and in tests their error rate on, for example, biomedical data can triple, or worse. We investigate techniques for building open-domain sequence labeling systems that approach the ideal of a system whose accuracy is high and constant across domains. In particular, we investigate unsupervised techniques for representation learning that provide new features which are stable across domains, in that they are predictive in both the training and out-of-domain test data. In experiments, our novel techniques reduce error by as much as 29% relative to the previous state of the art on out-of-domain text.

1 Introduction

Supervised natural language processing (NLP) systems exhibit a significant drop-off in performance when tested on domains that differ from their training domains. Past research in a variety of NLP tasks, like parsing (Gildea, 2001) and chunking (Huang and Yates, 2009), has shown that systems suffer from a drop-off in performance on out-of-domain tests. Two separate experiments with part-of-speech (POS) taggers trained on Wall Street Journal (WSJ) text show that they can reach accuracies of 97-98% on WSJ test sets, but achieve accuracies of at most 90% on biomedical text (R.Codena et al., 2005; Blitzer et al., 2006).

The major cause for poor performance on out-of-domain texts is the traditional representation used by supervised NLP systems. Most systems depend to varying degrees on lexical features, which tie predictions to the words observed in each example. While such features have been used in a variety of tasks for better in-domain performance, they are pitfalls for out-of-domain tests for two reasons: first, the vocabulary can differ greatly between domains, so that important words in the test data may never be seen in the training data. And second, the connection between words and labels may also change across domains. For instance, "signaling" appears only as a present participle (VBG) in WSJ text (as in, "signaling that ..."), but predominantly as a noun (as in "signaling pathway") in biomedical text.

Representation learning is a promising new approach to discovering useful features that are stable across domains. Blitzer *et al.* (2006) and our previous work (2009) demonstrate novel, unsupervised representation learning techniques that produce new features for domain adaptation of a POS tagger. This framework is attractive for several reasons: experimentally, learned features can yield significant improvements over standard supervised models on out-of-domain tests. Since the representation learning techniques are unsupervised, they can be applied to arbitrary new domains to yield the best set of features for learning on WSJ text and predicting on the new domain. There is no need to supply additional labeled examples for each new domain. This reduces the effort for domain adaptation, and makes it possible to apply systems to open-domain text collections like the Web, where it is prohibitively expensive to collect a labeled sample that is truly representative of all domains.

Here we explore two novel directions in the representation-learning framework for domain adaptation. Specifically, we investigate empirically the effects of representation learning techniques on POS tagging to answer the following:

Proceedings of the 2010 Workshop on Domain Adaptation for Natural Language Processing, ACL 2010, pages 23–30,
Uppsala, Sweden, 15 July 2010.

1. Can we produce multi-dimensional representations for domain adaptation? Our previous efforts have provided only a single new feature in the learned representations. We now show how we can perform a multi-dimensional clustering of words such that each dimension of the clustering forms a new feature in our representation; such multi-dimensional representations dramatically reduce the out-of-domain error rate of our POS tagger from 9.5% to 6.7%.
2. Can maximum-entropy models be used to produce representations for domain adaptation? Recent work on contrastive estimation (Smith and Eisner, 2005) has shown that maximum-entropy-based latent variable models can yield more accurate clusterings for POS tagging than more traditional generative models trained with Expectation-Maximization. Our preliminary results show that such models can be used effectively as representations for domain adaptation as well, matching state-of-the-art results while using far less data.

The next section provides background information on learning representations for NLP tasks using latent-variable language models. Section 3 describes our experimental setup. In Sections 4 and 5, we empirically investigate our two questions with a series of representation-learning methods. Section 6 analyzes our best learned representation to help explain its effectiveness. Section 7 presents previous work, and Section 8 concludes and outlines directions for future work.

2 Open-Domain Sequence Labeling by Learning Representations

Let $\mathcal{X}$ be an instance set for a learning problem; for POS tagging, for instance, this could be the set of all English sentences. Let $\mathcal{Y}$ be the space of possible labels for an instance, and let $f\colon \mathcal{X} \rightarrow \mathcal{Z}$ be the target function to be learned. A *representation* is a function $R\colon \mathcal{X} \rightarrow \mathcal{Y}$, for some suitable feature space $\mathcal{Y}$ (such as $\mathbb{R}^{\mathrm{d}}$). A *domain* is defined as a distribution $\mathcal{D}$ over the instance set $\mathcal{X}$. An open-domain system observes a set of training examples $(R(x), f(x))$, where instances $x \in \mathcal{X}$ are drawn from a *source* domain, to learn a hypothesis for classifying examples drawn from a separate *target* domain.

Previous work by Ben-David *et al.* (2007) uses Vapnik-Chervonenkis (VC) theory to show that the choice of representation is crucial to open-domain learning. As is customary in VC theory, a good choice of representation must allow a learning machine to achieve low error rates during training. Just as important, however, is that *the representation must simultaneously make the source and target domains look as similar to one another as possible.*

For open-domain sequence-labeling, then, the traditional representations are problematic. Typical representations in NLP use functions of the local context to produce features. Although many previous studies have shown that such lexical features allow learning systems to achieve impressively low error rates during training, they also make texts from different domains look very dissimilar. For instance, a sentence containing "bank" is almost certainly from the WSJ rather than biomedical text; a sentence containing "pathway" is almost certainly from a biomedical text rather than from the WSJ.

Our recent work (2009) shows how to build systems that learn new representations for open-domain NLP using latent-variable language models like Hidden Markov Models (HMMs). In POS-tagging and chunking experiments, these learned representations have proven to meet both of Ben-David *et al.*'s criteria for representations. They help discriminate among classes of words, since HMMs learn distributional similarity classes of words that often correlate with the labels that need to be predicted. Moreover, it would be difficult to tell apart two domains based on the set of HMM states that generated the texts, since a given HMM state may generate words from any number of domains.

In the rest of this paper, we investigate ways to improve the predictive power of the learned representations, without losing the essential property that the features remain stable across domains. We stay within the framework of using graphical models to learn representations, and demonstrate significant improvements on our original technique.

3 Experimental Setup

We use the same experimental setup as Blitzer *et al.* (2006): the Penn Treebank (Marcus et al., 1993) Wall Street Journal portion for our labeled training data; 561 MEDLINE sentences (9576 words) from the Penn BioIE project (PennBioIE, 2005) for our labeled test set; and all of the unlabeled text from the Penn Treebank WSJ portion plus Blitzer *et al.*'s MEDLINE corpus of 71,306 unlabeled sentences to train our latent variable models. The two texts come from two very different domains, making this data a tough test for domain adaptation. 23% of the word types in the test text are Out-Of-Vocabulary (OOV), meaning that they are never observed in the training data.

We use a number of unsupervised representation learning techniques to discover features from our unlabeled data, and a supervised classifier to train on the training set annotated with learned features. We use an open source Conditional Random Field (CRF) (Lafferty et al., 2001) software package[1] designed by Sunita Sajarwal and William W. Cohen to implement our supervised models. We refer to the baseline system with feature set following our previous work (2009) as PLAIN-CRF. Our learned features will supplement this set.

For comparison, we also report on the performance of Blitzer *et al.*'s Structural Correspondence Learning (SCL) (2006), our HMM-based model (2009)(HY09), and two other baselines:

- TEST-CRF: Our baseline model, trained and tested on the test data. This is our upper bound.
- SELF-CRF: Following the self-training paradigm (*e.g.*, (McClosky et al., 2006b; McClosky et al., 2006a)), we train our baseline first on the training set, then apply it to the test set, then retrain it on the training set plus the automatically labeled test set. We perform only one iteration of retraining, although in general multiple iterations are possible, usually with diminishing marginal returns.

4 Multi-dimensional Representations

From a linguistic perspective, words are multi-dimensional objects. For instance, the word "we" in "We like doing domain adaptation research" is a pronoun, a subject, first person, and plural, among other things. Each of these properties is a separate feature of this word, which can be changed without changing the other features. For example, if "we" is changed to "they" in the previous example, it is exactly the same as "we" in all aspects, except that it is third person; if "we" is changed to "us", then it changes from subject case to object case. In morphologically rich languages, many syntactic distinctions are marked in the surface forms of words; in more analytic or isolating languages like English, the distinctions are still there, but must often be inferred from context rather than word form. Beyond syntactic dimensions, numerous semantic properties can also distinguish words, such as nouns that refer to cognitive agents versus nouns that refer to materials and tools.

We seek to learn multidimensional representations of words. Our HMM-based model is able to categorize words in one dimension, by assigning a single HMM latent state to each word. Since the HMM is trained on unlabeled data, this dimension may partially reflect POS categories, but more likely represents a mixture of many different word dimensions. By adding in multiple hidden layers to our sequence model, we aim to learn a multi-dimensional representation that may help us to capture word features from multiple perspectives. The supervised CRF system can then sort out which dimensions are relevant to the sequence-labeling task at hand.

A Factorial HMM (FHMM) can be used to model multiple hidden dimensions of a word. However, the memory requirements of an FHMM increase exponentially with the number of layers in the graphical model, making it hard to use (see Table 1). Although other parameterizations may require much less memory, like using a log-linear output distribution conditioned on the factors, exact inference is still computationally intractable; exploring FHMMs with approximate inference and learning is an interesting area for future work. Here, we choose to create several single-layer HMMs separately. Figure 1 shows our Independent-HMM model (I-HMM). I-HMM has several copies of the observation sequence and each copy is associated with its own hidden label sequence. To encourage each layer of the I-HMM model to find a different local maximum in parameter space during training (and thus a different model of the observation sequence), we initialize the parameters randomly.

Suppose there are L independent layers in an I-HMM model for corpus $\mathbf{x} = (x_1, \ldots, x_N)$, and each layer is $(y_1^l, y_2^l, \ldots y_N^l)$, where $l = 1 \ldots L$ and each y can have K states. The distribution of the corpus and one hidden layer l is

$$P(\mathbf{x}, \mathbf{y^l}) = \prod_i P(x_i | y_i^l) P(y_i^l | y_{i-1}^l)$$

For each layer l, for each position i, each HMM

[1] Available from http://sourceforge.net/projects/crf/

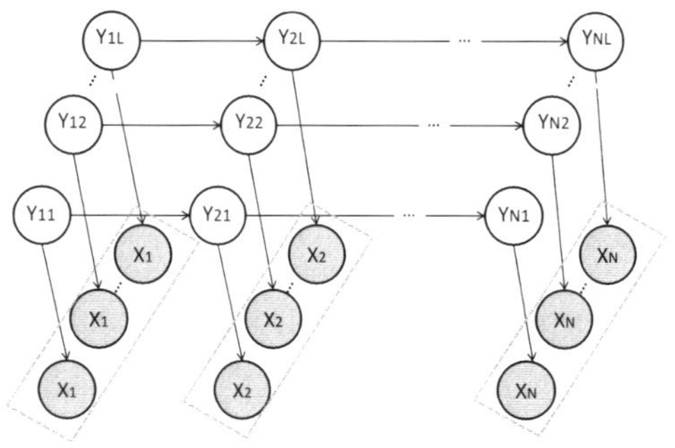

Figure 1: Graphical models of an Independent Hidden Markov Model. The dash line rectangle indicates that they are copies of the observation sequence

Model	Number of layers	Number of words	Number of states	Memory
HMM	1	W	K	$O(WK + K^2)$
FHMM	L	W	K	$O(WK^L + LK^2)$
I-HMM	L	W	K	$O(WKL + LK^2)$

Table 1: The memory requirement for HMM, FHMM, and I-HMM models.

state y and each POS tag z, we add a new boolean feature to our CRF system that indicates whether $Y_i^l = y$ and Z_i=z.

We experiment with two versions of I-HMM: first, we fix the number of states in each layer at 80 states, and increase the number of HMM layers from 1 to 8 (I-HMM(80)). Second, to provide greater encouragement for each layer to represent separate information, we vary the number of states in each layer (I-HMM(vary)). The detailed configuration for this model is shown in Table 2.

The results for our two models are shown in Figure 2. We can see that the accuracy of I-HMM(80) model keeps increasing from 90.5% to 93.3% until 7 layers of HMM features (we call this 7-layer representation I-HMM*). This is a dramatic 29% decrease in the best reported error rate for this dataset when no labeled data from the biomedical domain is used. Unlike with an FHMM, there is no guarantee that the different layers of an I-HMM will model different aspects of the observation signal, but our results indicate that for at least several layers, the induced models are complementary. After 7 layers, results begin to decrease, most likely because the added layer is no longer complementary to the existing latent-variable models and is causing the supervised CRF to overfit the training data.

For the I-HMM(vary) model with up to 5 layers, the accuracy is not as good as I-HMM(80), although the 5-layer model still outperforms HY09. Individually, HMM models with fewer than 80 states perform worse than the 80-state model (a model with 40 states achieved 89.4% accuracy, and a model with 20 states achieved 88.9%). We had hoped that by using layers with different numbers of states, we could force the layers to learn complementary models, but the results indicate that any benefit from complementarity is outweighed by the lower performance of the individual layers.

Number of Layers	Number of States in each Layer
1	10
2	10 20
3	10 20 40
4	10 20 40 60
5	10 20 40 60 80

Table 2: The configuration of HMM layers and HMM states for the I-HMM(vary) model

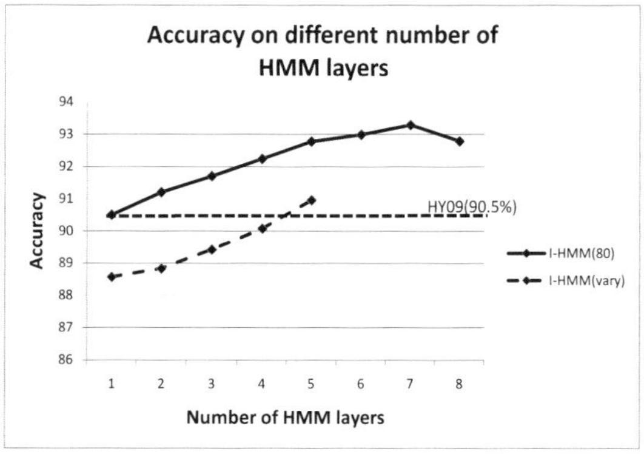

Figure 2: Our best multi-dimensional smoothed-HMM tagger with 7 layers reaches 93.3% accuracy, a drop of nearly 3% in the error rate from the previous state of the art (HY09).

5 Learning Representations with Contrastive Estimation

In recent years, many NLP practitioners have begun using discriminative models, and especially maximum-entropy-based models like CRFs, because they allow the modeler to incorporate arbitrary, interacting features of the observation sequence while still providing tractable inference. To see if the same benefit can carry over to our representation learning, we aim to build maximum-entropy-based linear-chain models that, unlike most discriminative models, train on unannotated data. We follow Smith and Eisner (2005) in training our models using a technique called *contrastive estimation*, which we explain below. We call the resulting model the Smith and Eisner Model (SEM).

The key to SEM is that the contrastive estimation training procedure forces the model to explain why the given training data are better than perturbed versions of the data, called neighbor points. For example, the sentence "We like doing domain adaptation research" is a valid sentence, but if we switched "like" and "doing", the new sentence "We doing like domain adaptation research" is not valid. SEM learns a model of the original sentence by contrasting it with the invalid neighbor sentences.

Let $\vec{x} =< x_1, x_2, ..., x_N >$ be the observed example sentences, and let $\mathcal{Y}$ be the space of possible hidden structures for x_i. Let $\mathcal{N}(x_i)$ be a "neighborhood" for x_i, or a set of negative examples obtained by perturbing x_i, plus x_i itself. Given a vector of feature functions $\vec{f}(x, y)$, SEM tries to find a set of weights $\vec{\theta}$ that maximize a log-likelihood function:

$$\mathcal{L}_{\mathcal{N}}(\vec{\theta}) = log \prod_i \frac{\sum_{y \in \mathcal{Y}} u(x_i, y|\vec{\theta})}{\sum_{(x,y) \in \mathcal{N}(x_i) \times \mathcal{Y}} u(x, y|\vec{\theta})}$$

where $u(x, y|\vec{\theta}) = \exp(\vec{\theta} \cdot \vec{f}(x, y))$ is the "unnormalized probability" of an (example, hidden structure) pair (x,y). Following Smith and Eisner, we use the best performing neighborhood, called TRANS1, to conduct our experiments. TRANS1 is the set of sentences resulting from transposing any pair of adjacent words for any given training example.

The base feature space for SEM includes two kinds of boolean features analogous to HMM emission and transition probabilities. For an observation sequence $x_1, \ldots, x_T$ and a label sequence $y_1, \ldots, y_T$, a boolean emission feature indicates whether $x_t = x$ and $y_t = y$ for all possible t, x, and y. A boolean transition feature indicates whether $y_{t-1} = y$ and $y_t = y'$ for all possible t, y, and y'.

Because contrastive estimation is a computationally expensive training procedure, we take two steps to reduce the computational cost: we reduce the unlabeled data set, and we prune the feature set of SEM. For our training data, we use only the sentences with length less than or equal to 10. We also get rid of punctuation and the corresponding tags, change all words to lowercase and change all numbers into a single symbol.

To reduce the feature space, we create a tagging dictionary from Penn Treebank sections 02-21: for every word in these sections, the dictionary records the set of POS tags that were ever associated with that word. We then prune the emission features for words that appear in this dictionary to include only the features that associate words with their corresponding POS tags in the dictionary. For the words that don't appear in the Penn Treebank, they are associated with all possible POS tags. This procedure reduces the total number of features in our SEM model from over 500,000 to just over 60,000.

After we train the model, we use a Viterbi-like algorithm to decode it on the testing set. Unlike the HMM model, the decoded states of SEM are already meaningful POS tags, so we can use these decoded states as POS tags (PLAIN-SEM), or use them as features for a CRF model (SEM-CRF). We show the result of both models, as well as several comparison models, in Table 3. From the result, we can see that the unsupervised PLAIN-SEM outperforms the supervised PLAIN-CRF on both all words and OOV words. This impressive performance results from its ability to adapt to the new domain through the unlabeled training examples and the contrastive estimation training procedure. In addition, the SEM-CRF model significantly outperforms the SCL model (88.9%) and the HMM-based CRF with 40 hidden states (89.4%) while using only 36 hidden states, although it does not quite reach the performance of HY09. These results, which use a subset of the available unlabeled training text, suggest that maximum-entropy-style representation learning is a promising area for further investigation.

6 Analysis

As we mention in Section 2, the choice of representation is crucial to open-domain learning. In Sections 4 and 5, we demonstrate empirically that learned representations based on latent-variable graphical models can significantly improve the accuracy of a POS tagger on a new domain, compared with using the traditional word-level representations. We now examine our best representation, I-HMM*, in light of the theoretical predictions made by VC theory.

Model	All words	OOV words
PLAIN-CRF	88.3	67.3
SELF-CRF	88.5	70.4
PLAIN-SEM	88.5	69.8
SCL	88.9	72.0
SEM-CRF	90.0	71.9
HY09	90.5	75.2
I-HMM*	**93.3**	**76.3**
TEST-CRF	98.9	NA

Table 3: SEM-CRF reduces error compared with SCL by 1.1% on all words; I-HMM* closes 33% of the gap between the state-of-the-art HY09 and the upper-bound, TEST-CRF.

In particular, Ben-David *et al.*'s analysis shows that the distance between two domains under a representation R of the data is crucial to domain adaptation. However, their analysis depends on a particular notion of distance, the $\mathcal{H}$-divergence, that is computationally intractable to calculate. For our analysis, we resort instead to a crude but telling approximation of this measure, using a more standard notion of distance: Jensen-Shannon Divergence (D_{JS}).

To calculate the distance between domains under a representation R, we represent a domain D as a multinomial probability distribution over the set of features in R. We take maximum-likelihood estimates of this distribution using our samples from the WSJ and MEDLINE domains. We then measure the Jensen-Shannon Divergence between the two distributions, which for discrete distributions is calculated as

$$D_{JS}(p||q) = \frac{1}{2}\sum_i \left[p_i \log\left(\frac{p_i}{m_i}\right) + q_i \log\left(\frac{q_i}{m_i}\right)\right]$$

where $m = \frac{p+q}{2}$.

Figure 3 shows the divergence between these two domains under purely lexical features, and under only HMM-based features. OOV words make up a substantial portion of the divergence between the two domains under the lexical representation, but even if we ignore them the HMM features are substantially less variable across the two domains, which helps to explain their ability to provide supervised classifiers with stable features for domain adaptation. Because there are so few HMM states compared with the number of word types, there is no such thing as an OOV HMM state, and the word states that appear in training data appear roughly as often in test data. This means that any associations that the CRF might learn between HMM states and predicted outcomes is likely to remain useful on the test data, but associations between words and outcomes are less likely to be useful.

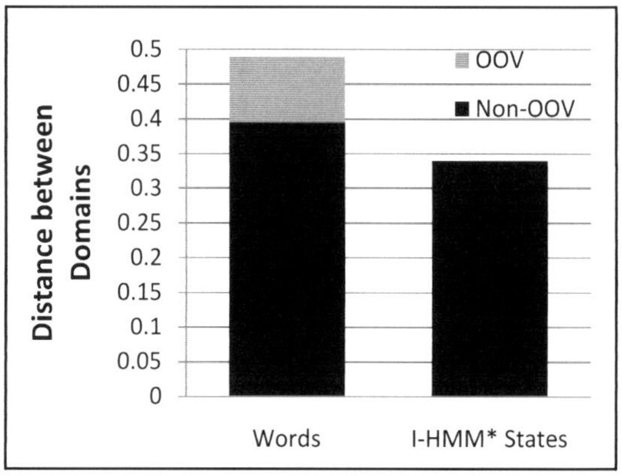

Figure 3: The Jensen-Shannon Divergence between the newswire domain and the biomedical domain, according to a word-based representation of the domains and a HMM-based representation. The portion of the distance that is due to words which appear in the biomedical domain but not the newswire domain is shown in gray.

7 Previous Work

Previous work on artificial neural networks (ANNs) (Fahlman and Lebiere, 1990) has shown that it is possible to learn effectively by adding more hidden units to the neural network that correlate with the residual error of the existing hidden units (Cascade-Correlation learning). Like our I-HMM technique, this work aims to build a multi-dimensional model, and it is capable of learning the number of appropriate dimensions. Unlike the ANN scenario, our multi-dimensional learning techniques must handle unlabeled data, and they rely on the sequential structure of language to learn effectively, whereas Cascade-Correlation learning assumes samples are independent and identically distributed. Our techniques do not (yet) automatically determine the best number of layers in the model.

Unlike our techniques for domain adaptation, in most cases researchers have focused on the scenario where labeled training data is available in both the source and the target domain (*e.g.*, (Bacchiani et al., 2006; Daumé III, 2007; Chelba and

Acero, 2004; Daumé III and Marcu, 2006; Blitzer et al., 2007)). Our techniques use only raw text from the target domain. This reduces the cost of domain adaptation and makes the techniques more widely applicable to new domains like web processing, where the domain and vocabulary is highly variable, and it is extremely difficult to obtain labeled data that is representative of the test distribution. When labeled target-domain data is available, instance weighting and similar techniques can potentially be used in combination with our techniques to improve our results further.

Several researchers have previously studied methods for using unlabeled data for sequence labeling, either alone or as a supplement to labeled data. Ando and Zhang develop a semi-supervised chunker that outperforms purely supervised approaches on the CoNLL 2000 dataset (Ando and Zhang, 2005). Recent projects in semi-supervised (Toutanova and Johnson, 2007) and unsupervised (Biemann et al., 2007; Smith and Eisner, 2005) tagging also show significant progress. HMMs have been used many times for POS tagging in supervised, semi-supervised, and in unsupervised settings (Banko and Moore, 2004; Goldwater and Griffiths, 2007; Johnson, 2007). The REALM system for sparse information extraction has also used unsupervised HMMs to help determine whether the arguments of a candidate relation are of the appropriate type (Downey et al., 2007). Schütze (1994) has presented an algorithm that categorizes word tokens in context instead of word types for tagging words. We take a novel perspective on the use of unsupervised latent-variable models by using them to compute features of each token that represent the distribution over that token's contexts. These features prove to be highly useful for supervised sequence labelers in out-of-domain tests.

In the deep learning (Bengio, 2009) paradigm, researchers have investigated multi-layer latent-variable models for language modeling, among other tasks. While n-gram models have traditionally dominated in language modeling, two recent efforts develop latent-variable probabilistic models that rival and even surpass n-gram models in accuracy (Blitzer et al., 2005; Mnih and Hinton, 2007). Several authors investigate neural network models that learn a vector of latent variables to represent each word (Bengio et al., 2003; Emami et al., 2003; Morin and Bengio, 2005). And factorial Hidden Markov Models (Ghahramani and Jordan, 1997) are a multi-layer variant of the HMM that has been used in speech recognition, among other things. We use simpler mixtures of single-layer models for the sake of memory-efficiency, and we use our models as representations in a supervised task, rather than as language models.

8 Conclusion and Future Work

Our representation learning approach to domain adaptation yields state-of-the-art results in POS tagging experiments. Our best models use multi-dimensional clustering to find several latent categories for each word; the latent categories serve as useful and domain-independent features for our supervised learner. Our exploration has yielded significant progress already, but it has only scratched the surface of possible models for this task. The current representation learning techniques we use are unsupervised, meaning that they provide the same set of categories, regardless of what task they are to be used for. Semi-supervised learning approaches could be developed to guide the representation learning process towards features that are best-suited for a particular task, but are still useful across domains. Our current approach also requires retraining of a CRF for every new domain; incremental retraining techniques for new domains would speed up the process and make domain adaptation much more accessible. Finally, there are cases where small amounts of labeled data are available for new domains; models that combine our representation learning approach with instance weighting and other forms of supervised domain adaptation may take better advantage of these cases.

Acknowledgments

We wish to thank the anonymous reviewers for their helpful comments and suggestions.

References

Rie Kubota Ando and Tong Zhang. 2005. A high-performance semi-supervised learning method for text chunking. In *ACL*.

Michiel Bacchiani, Michael Riley, Brian Roark, and Richard Sproat. 2006. MAP adaptation of stochastic grammars. *Computer Speech and Language*, 20(1):41–68.

Michele Banko and Robert C. Moore. 2004. Part of speech tagging in context. In *COLING*.

Shai Ben-David, John Blitzer, Koby Crammer, and Fernando Pereira. 2007. Analysis of representations for domain adaptation. In *Advances in Neural Information Processing Systems 20*, Cambridge, MA. MIT Press.

Yoshua Bengio, Réjean Ducharme, Pascal Vincent, and Christian Janvin. 2003. A neural probabilistic language model. *Journal of Machine Learning Research*, 3:1137–1155.

Y. Bengio. 2009. Learning deep architectures for AI. *Foundations and Trends in Machine Learning*, 2.

C. Biemann, C. Giuliano, and A. Gliozzo. 2007. Unsupervised pos tagging supporting supervised methods. *Proceeding of RANLP-07*.

J. Blitzer, A. Globerson, and F. Pereira. 2005. Distributed latent variable models of lexical cooccurrences. In *Proceedings of the Tenth International Workshop on Artificial Intelligence and Statistics*.

John Blitzer, Ryan McDonald, and Fernando Pereira. 2006. Domain adaptation with structural correspondence learning. In *EMNLP*.

John Blitzer, Koby Crammer, Alex Kulesza, Fernando Pereira, and Jenn Wortman. 2007. Learning bounds for domain adaptation. In *Advances in Neural Information Processing Systems*.

Ciprian Chelba and Alex Acero. 2004. Adaptation of maximum entropy classifier: Little data can help a lot. In *EMNLP*.

Hal Daumé III and Daniel Marcu. 2006. Domain adaptation for statistical classifiers. *Journal of Artificial Intelligence Research*, 26.

Hal Daumé III. 2007. Frustratingly easy domain adaptation. In *ACL*.

Doug Downey, Stefan Schoenmackers, and Oren Etzioni. 2007. Sparse information extraction: Unsupervised language models to the rescue. In *ACL*.

A. Emami, P. Xu, and F. Jelinek. 2003. Using a connectionist model in a syntactical based language model. In *Proceedings of the International Conference on Spoken Language Processing*, pages 372–375.

Scott E. Fahlman and Christian Lebiere. 1990. The cascade-correlation learning architecture. *Advances in Neural Information Processing Systems 2*.

Zoubin Ghahramani and Michael I. Jordan. 1997. Factorial hidden markov models. *Machine Learning*, 29(2-3):245–273.

Daniel Gildea. 2001. Corpus Variation and Parser Performance. In *Conference on Empirical Methods in Natural Language Processing*.

Sharon Goldwater and Thomas L. Griffiths. 2007. A fully bayesian approach to unsupervised part-of-speech tagging. In *ACL*.

Fei Huang and Alexander Yates. 2009. Distributional representations for handling sparsity in supervised sequence labeling. In *Proceedings of the Annual Meeting of the Association for Computational Linguistics*.

Mark Johnson. 2007. Why doesn't EM find good HMM POS-taggers. In *EMNLP*.

J. Lafferty, Andrew McCallum, and Fernando Pereira. 2001. Conditional random fields: Probabilistic models for segmenting and labeling sequence data. In *Proceedings of the International Conference on Machine Learning*.

Mitchell P. Marcus, Mary Ann Marcinkiewicz, and Beatrice Santorini. 1993. Building a large annotated corpus of English: the Penn Treebank. *Computational Linguistics*, 19(2):313–330.

David McClosky, Eugene Charniak, and Mark Johnson. 2006a. Effective self-training for parsing. In *Proc. of HLT-NAACL*.

David McClosky, Eugene Charniak, and Mark Johnson. 2006b. Reranking and self-training for parser adaptation. In *Proceedings of the 21st International Conference on Computational Linguistics and 44th Annual Meeting of the ACL*, pages 337–344.

Andriy Mnih and Geoffrey Hinton. 2007. Three new graphical models for statistical language modelling. In *Proceedings of the 24th International Conference on Machine Learning*, pages 641–648, New York, NY, USA. ACM.

F. Morin and Y. Bengio. 2005. Hierarchical probabilistic neural network language model. In *Proceedings of the International Workshop on Artificial Intelligence and Statistics*, pages 246–252.

PennBioIE. 2005. Mining the bibliome project. *http://bioie.ldc.upenn.edu/*.

Anni R.Codena, Serguei V.Pakhomovb, Rie K.Andoa, Patrick H.Duffyb, and Christopher G.Chute. 2005. Domain-specific language models and lexicons for tagging. *Journal of Biomedical Informatics*, 38(6):422–430.

Hinrich Schütze. 1994. Distributional part-of-speech tagging. In *Proceedings of the 7th Conference of the European Chapter of the Association for Computational Linguistics (EACL)*.

Noah A. Smith and Jason Eisner. 2005. Contrastive estimation: Training log-linear models on unlabeled data. In *Proceedings of the 43rd Annual Meeting of the Association for Computational Linguistics (ACL)*, pages 354–362, Ann Arbor, Michigan, June.

Kristina Toutanova and Mark Johnson. 2007. A bayesian LDA-based model for semi-supervised part-of-speech tagging. In *NIPS*.

Using Domain Similarity for Performance Estimation

Vincent Van Asch
CLiPS - University of Antwerp
Antwerp, Belgium
Vincent.VanAsch@ua.ac.be

Walter Daelemans
CLiPS - University of Antwerp
Antwerp, Belgium
Walter.Daelemans@ua.ac.be

Abstract

Many natural language processing (NLP) tools exhibit a decrease in performance when they are applied to data that is linguistically different from the corpus used during development. This makes it hard to develop NLP tools for domains for which annotated corpora are not available. This paper explores a number of metrics that attempt to predict the cross-domain performance of an NLP tool through statistical inference. We apply different similarity metrics to compare different domains and investigate the correlation between similarity and accuracy loss of NLP tool. We find that the correlation between the performance of the tool and the similarity metric is linear and that the latter can therefore be used to predict the performance of an NLP tool on out-of-domain data. The approach also provides a way to quantify the difference between domains.

1 Introduction

Domain adaptation has recently turned into a broad field of study (Bellegarda, 2004). Many researchers note that the linguistic variation between training and testing corpora is an important factor in assessing the performance of an NLP tool across domains. For example, a tool that has been developed to extract predicate-argument structures from abstracts of biomedical research papers, will exhibit a lower performance when applied to legal texts.

However, the notion of *domain* is mostly arbitrarily used to refer to some kind of semantic area. There is unfortunately no unambiguous measure to assert a domain shift, except by observing the performance loss of an NLP tool when applied across different domains. This means that we typically need annotated data to reveal a domain shift. In this paper we will show how unannotated data can be used to get a clearer view on how datasets differ. This unsupervised way of looking at data will give us a method to measure the difference between data sets and allows us to predict the performance of an NLP tool on unseen, out-of-domain data.

In Section 2 we will explain our approach in detail. In Section 3 we deal with a case study involving basic part-of-speech taggers, applied to different domains. An overview of related work can be found in Section 4. Finally, Section 5 concludes this paper and discusses options for further research.

2 Approach

When developing an NLP tool using supervised learning, annotated data with the same linguistic properties as the data for which the tool is developed is needed, but not always available. In many cases, this means that the developer needs to collect and annotate data suited for the task. When this is not possible, it would be useful to have a method that can estimate the performance on corpus B of an NLP tool trained on corpus A in an unsupervised way, i.e., without the necessity to annotate a part of B.

In order to be able to predict in an unsupervised way the performance of an NLP tool on different corpora, we need a way to measure the differences between the corpora. The metric at hand should be independent from the annotation labels, so that it can be easily applied on any given corpus. The aim is to find a metric such that the correlation between the metric and the performance is statistically significant. In the scope of this article the concept *metric* stands for any way of assigning a sufficiently fine-grained label to a corpus, using only unannotated data. This means that, in our view, a metric can be an elaborate mixture of frequency counts, rules, syntactic pattern matching or

Proceedings of the 2010 Workshop on Domain Adaptation for Natural Language Processing, ACL 2010, pages 31–36,
Uppsala, Sweden, 15 July 2010.

even machine learner driven tools. However, in the remainder of this paper we will only look at frequency based similarity metrics since these metrics are easily applicable and the experiments conducted using these metrics were already encouraging.

3 Experimental design

3.1 Corpus

We used data extracted from the British National Corpus (BNC) (2001) and consisting of written books and periodicals[1]. The BNC annotators provided 9 domain codes (i.e. wridom), making it possible to divide the text from books and periodicals into 9 subcorpora. These annotated semantic domains are: imaginative (wridom1), natural & pure science (wridom2), applied science (wridom3), social science (wridom4), world affairs (wridom5), commerce & finance (wridom6), arts (wridom7), belief & thought (wridom8), and leisure (wridom9).

The extracted corpus contains sentences in which every token is tagged with a part-of-speech tag as defined by the BNC. Since the BNC has been tagged automatically, using the CLAWS4 automatic tagger (Leech *et al.*, 1994) and the Template Tagger (Pacey *et al.*, 1997), the experiments in this article are artificial in the sense that they do not learn *real* part-of-speech tags but rather part-of-speech tags as they are assigned by the automatic taggers.

3.2 Similarity metrics

To measure the difference between two corpora we implemented six similarity metrics: Rényi[2] (Rényi, 1961), Variational (L1) (Lee, 2001), Euclidean (Lee, 2001), Cosine (Lee, 2001), Kullback-Leibler (Kullback and Leibler, 1951) and Bhattacharyya coefficient (Comaniciu *et al.*, 2003; Bhattacharyya, 1943). We selected these measures because they are well-described and produce results for this task in an acceptable time span.

The metrics are computed using the relative frequencies of words. For example, to calculate the Rényi divergence between corpus P and corpus Q the following formula is applied:

$$Rényi(P;Q;\alpha) = \frac{1}{(\alpha-1)} log_2 \left(\sum^k p_k^{1-\alpha} q_k^{\alpha} \right)$$

p_k is the relative frequency of a token k in the first corpus P, and q_k is the relative frequency of token k in the second corpus Q. α is a free parameter and with $\alpha = 1$ the Rényi divergence becomes equivalent to the Kullback-Leibler divergence.

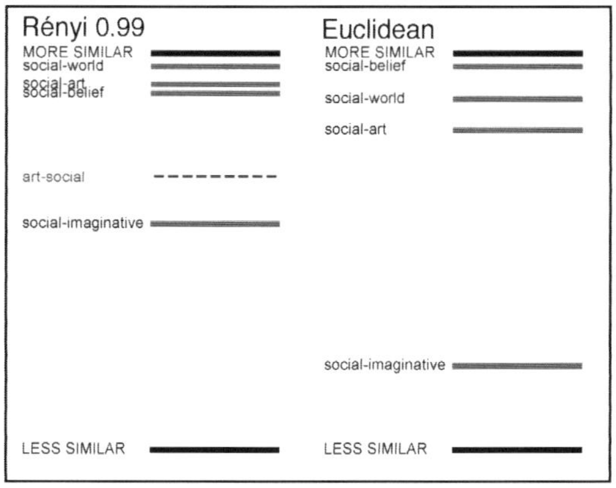

Figure 1: A visual comparison of two similarity metrics: Rényi with $\alpha = 0.99$ and Euclidean.

Figure 1 gives an impression of the difference between two similarity metrics: Rényi ($\alpha = 0.99$) and Euclidean. Only four domain combinations are shown for the sake of clarity. From the graph it can be observed that the *social* and *imaginative* domains are the least similar in both cases. Besides the different ordering, there is also a difference in symmetry. Contrary to the symmetric Euclidean metric, the Rényi scores differ, depending on whether *social* constitutes the test set and *art* the training set, or vice versa. The dashed line on Figure 1 (left) is a reverse score, namely for *art-social*. A divergence score may diverge a lot from its reverse score.

In practice, the best metric to choose is the metric that gives the best linear correlation between the metric and the accuracy of an NLP tool applied across domains. We tested 6 metrics: Rényi, Variational (L1), Euclidean, Cosine, Kullback-Leibler, and the Bhattacharyya coefficient. For Rényi, we tested four different α-values: 0.95, 0.99, 1.05, and 1.1. Most metrics gave a linear correlation but for our experiments with data-driven POS tagging, the Rényi metric with $\alpha = 0.99$ was the best

[1] This is done by selecting texts with BNC category codes for text type (i.e. alltyp3 (written books and periodicals)) and for medium (i.e. wrimed1 (book), wrimed2 (periodical), and wrimed3 (miscellaneous: published)).

[2] The Rényi divergence has a parameter α and Kullback-Leibler is a special case of the Rényi divergence, viz. with $\alpha = 1$.

according to the Pearson product-moment correlation. For majority this correlation was 0.91, for Mbt 0.93, and for SVMTool 0.93.

3.3 Part-of-speech tagging

The experiments carried out in the scope of this article are all part-of-speech (POS) tagging tasks. There are 91 different POS labels in the BNC corpus which are combinations of 57 basic labels. We used three algorithms to assign part-of-speech labels to the words from the test corpus:

Majority This algorithm assigns the POS label that occurs most frequently in the training set for a given word, to the word in the test set. If the word did not occur in train, the overall most frequent tag was used.

Memory based POS tagger (Daelemans and van den Bosch, 2005) A machine learner that stores examples in memory (Mbt) and uses the *k*NN algorithm to assign POS labels. The default settings were used.

SVMTool POS tagger (Giménez and Márquez, 2004) Support vectors machines in a sequential setup are used to assign the POS labels. The default settings were used.

3.4 Results and analysis

Figure 2 shows the outcome of 72 cross-validation experiments on the data from the British National Corpus. The graph for the majority baseline is shown in Figure 2a. The results for the memory based tagger are shown in Figure 2b and the graph for SVMTool is displayed in Figure 2c.

For every domain, the data is divided into five parts. For all pairs of domains, each part from the training domain is paired with each part from the testing domain. This results in a 25 cross-validation cross-domain experiment. A data point in Figure 2 is the average outcome of such a 25 fold experiment. The abscissa of a data point is the Rényi similarity score between the training and testing component of an experiment. The α parameter was set to 0.99. We propose that the higher (less negative) the similarity score, the more similar training and testing data are.

The ordinate is the accuracy of the POS tagging experiment. The dotted lines are the 95% prediction intervals for every data point. These boundaries are obtained by linear regression using all other data points. The interpretation of the intervals is that any point, given all other data points

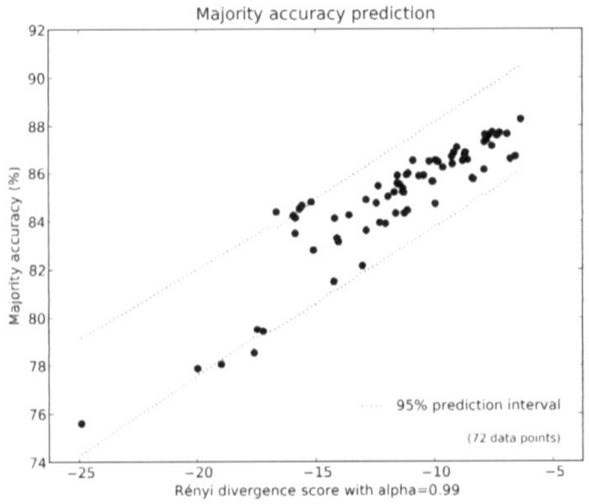

(a) Majority POS tagger.

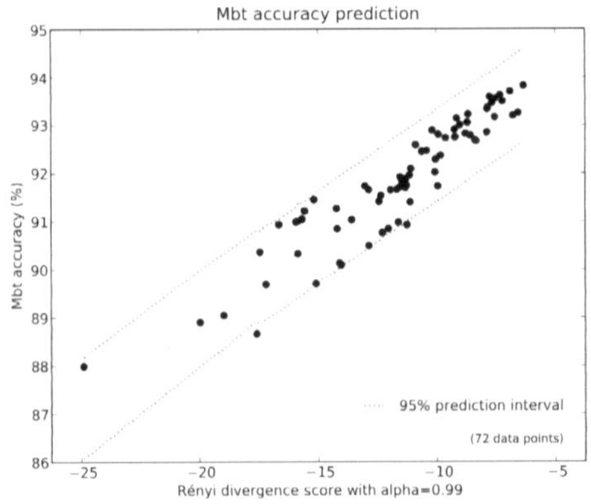

(b) Memory based POS tagger.

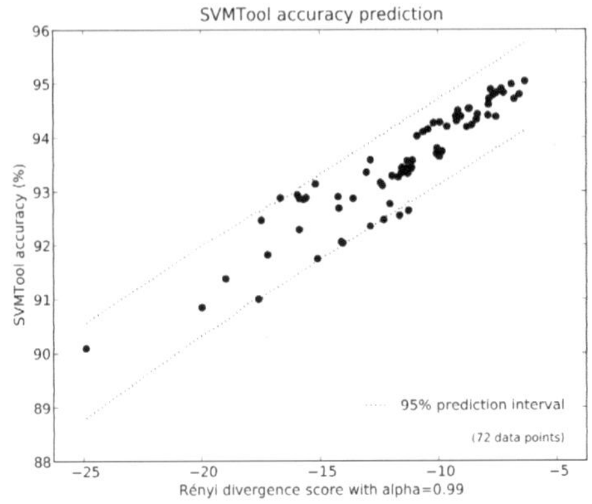

(c) SVMTool POS tagger.

Figure 2: The varying accuracy of three POS taggers with varying distance between train and test corpus of different domains.

from the graph, can be predicted with 95% certainty, to lie between the upper and lower interval boundary at the similarity score of that point. The average difference between the lower and the upper interval boundary is 4.36% for majority, 1.92% for Mbt and 1.59% for SVMTool. This means that,

	Majority	Mbt	SVMTool
average accuracy	84.94	91.84	93.48
standard deviation	2.50	1.30	1.07

Table 1: Average accuracy and standard deviation on 72 cross-validation experiments.

when taking the middle of the interval as the expected accuracy, the maximum error is 0.8% for SVMTool. Since the difference between the best and worst accuracy score is 4.93%, using linear regression means that one can predict the accuracy three times better. For Mbt with a range of 5.84% between best and worst accuracy and for majority with 12.7%, a similar figure is obtained.

Table 1 shows the average accuracies of the algorithms for all 72 experiments. For this article, the absolute accuracy of the algorithms is not under consideration. Therefore, no effort has been made to improve on these accuracy scores. One can see that the standard deviation for SVMTool and Mbt is lower than for majority, suggesting that these algorithms are less susceptible to domain variation.

The good linear fit for the graphs of Figure 2 cannot be reproduced with every algorithm. For algorithms that do not have a sufficiently strong relation between training corpus and assigned class label, the linear relation is lost. Clearly, it remains feasible to compute an interval for the data points, but as a consequence of the non-linearity, the predicted intervals would be similar or even bigger than the difference between the lowest and highest accuracy score.

In Figure 3 the experiments of Figure 2 are reproduced using test and training sets from the same domain. Since we used the same data sets as for the out-of-domain experiments, we had to carry out 20 fold cross-validation for these experiments. Because of this different setup the results are shown in a different figure. There is a data point for every domain.

Although the average distance between test and training set are smaller for in-domain experiments, we still observe a linear relation for Mbt and SVM, for majority there is still a visual hint of linearity. For in-domain the biggest difference between test and train set is for the *leisure* domain (Rényi score: -6.0) which is very close to the smallest out-of-domain difference (-6.3 for social sciences–world affairs). This could mean that the random variation between test and train can approach the varia-

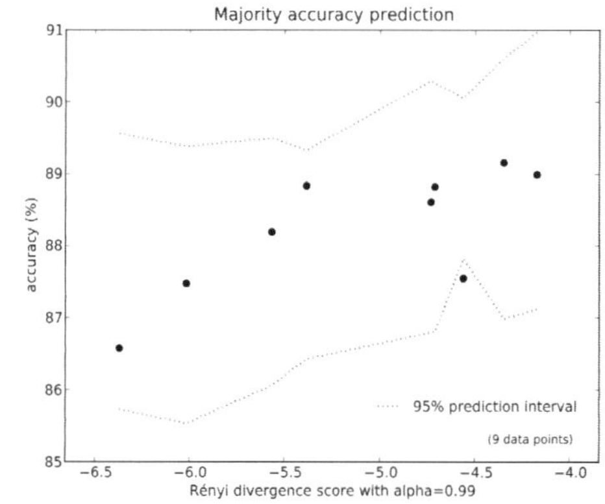

(a) Majority POS tagger.

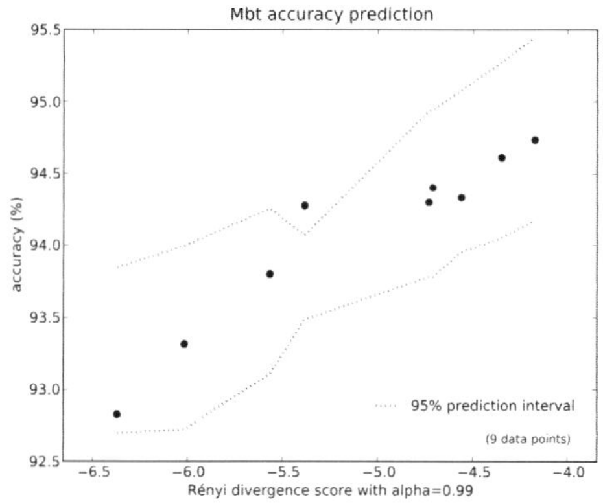

(b) Memory based POS tagger.

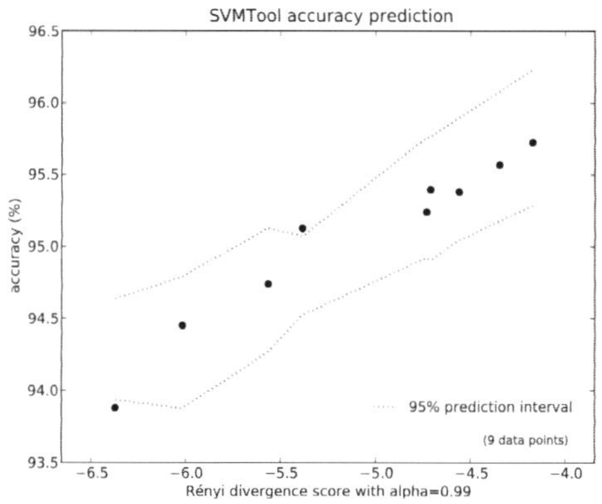

(c) SVMTool POS tagger.

Figure 3: The varying accuracy of three POS taggers with varying distance between train and test corpus of the same domain.

tion between domains but this observation is made in abstraction from the different data set sizes for in and out of domain experiments. For majority the average accuracy over all domains is 88.25% (stdev: 0.87), for Mbt 94.07% (0.63), and for SVMTool 95.06% (0.59). Which are, as expected, higher scores than the figures in Table 1.

4 Related Work

In articles dealing with the influence of domain shifts on the performance of an NLP tool, the in-domain data and out-of-domain data are taken from different corpora, e.g., sentences from movie snippets, newspaper texts and personal weblogs (Andreevskaia and Bergler, 2008). It can be expected that these corpora are indeed dissimilar enough to consider them as separate domains, but no objective measure has been used to define them as such. The fact that the NLP tool produces lower results for cross-domain experiments can be taken as an indication of the presence of separate domains. A nice overview paper on statistical domain adaptation can be found in Bellegarda (2004).

A way to express the degree of relatedness, apart from this well-known accuracy drop, can be found in Daumé and Marcu (2006). They propose a domain adaptation framework containing a parameter π. Low values of π mean that in-domain and out-of-domain data differ significantly. They also used Kullback-Leibler divergence to compute the similarity between unigram language models.

Blitzer *et al.* (2007) propose a supervised way of measuring the similarity between the two domains. They compute the Huber loss, as a proxy of the $\mathcal{A}$-distance (Kifer *et al.*, 2004), for every instance that they labeled with their tool. The resulting measure correlates with the adaptation loss they observe when applying a sentiment classification tool on different domains.

5 Conclusions and future work

This paper showed that it is possible to narrow down the prediction of the accuracy of an NLP tool on an unannotated corpus by measuring the similarity between this unannotated corpus and the corpus the tagger was trained on in an unsupervised way. A prerequisite to be able to make a reliable prediction, is to have sufficient annotated data to measure the correlation between the accuracy and a metric. We observed that, in order to make a prediction interval that is narrower than the difference between the lowest and highest accuracy on the annotated corpora, the algorithm used, should capture sufficient information from training.

The observation that it is feasible to make reliable predictions using unannotated data, can be of help when training a system for a task in a domain for which no annotated data is available. As a first step, the metric resulting in the best linear fit between the metric and the accuracy should be searched. If a linear relation can be established, one can take annotated training data from the domain that is closest to the unannotated corpus and assume that this will give the best accuracy score.

In this article we implemented a way to measure the similarity between two corpora. One may decide to use such a metric to categorize the available corpora for a given task into groups, depending on their similarity. It should be noted that in order to do this, a symmetric metric should be used. Indeed, an asymmetric metric like the Rényi divergence will give a different value depending on whether the similarity between corpus P and corpus Q is measured as $Rényi(P;Q;\alpha)$ or as $Rényi(Q;P;\alpha)$.

Further research should explore the usability of linear regression for other NLP tasks. Although no specific adaptation to the POS tagging task was made, it may not be straightforward to find a linear relation for more complicated tasks. For such tasks, it may be useful to insert n-grams into the metric. Or, if a parser was first applied to the data, it is possible to insert syntactic features in the metric. Of course, these adaptations may influence the efficiency of the metric, but if a good linear relation between the metric and the accuracy can be found, the metric is useful. Another option to make the use of the metric less task dependent is by not using the distribution of the tokens but by using distributions of the features used by the machine learner. Applying this more generic setup of our experiments to other NLP tools may lead to the discovery of a metric that is generally applicable.

Acknowledgments

This research was made possible through financial support from the University of Antwerp (BIOGRAPH GOA-project).

References

Alfred V. Aho and Jeffrey D. Ullman. 1972. *The Theory of Parsing, Translation and Compiling*, volume 1. Prentice-Hall, Englewood Cliffs, NJ.

Alina Andreevskaia and Sabine Bergler. 2008. When Specialists and Generalists Work Together: Overcoming Domain Dependence in Sentiment Tagging. *Proceedings of the 46th Annual Meeting of the Association for Computational Linguistics: Human Language Technologies (ACL-08:HLT)*, 290–298. Association for Computational Linguistics. Columbus, Ohio, USA.

Jerome R. Bellegarda. 2004. Statistical language model adaptation: review and perspectives. *Speech Communication*, 42:93–108.

Anil Bhattacharyya. 1943. On a measure of divergence between two statistical populations defined by their probability distributions. *Bulletin of the Calcutta Mathematical Society*, 35:99–109.

John Blitzer, Mark Dredze, and Fernando Pereira. 2007. Biographies, Bollywood, Boom-boxes and Blenders: Domain Adaptation for Sentiment Classification. *Proceedings of the 45th Annual Meeting of the Association of Computational Linguistics*, 440–447. Association for Computational Linguistics. Prague, Czech Republic.

British National Corpus Consortium. 2001. The British National Corpus, version 2 (BNC World). Distributed by Oxford University Computing Services on behalf of the BNC Consortium. http://www.natcorp.ox.ac.uk (Last accessed: April 2, 2010).

Dorin Comaniciu, Visvanathan Ramesh, and Peter Meer. 2003. Kernel-Based Object Tracking. *IEEE Transactions on Pattern Analysis and Machine Intelligence*, 25(5):564–575.

Walter Daelemans and Antal van den Bosch. 2005. *Memory-Based Language Processing*. Cambridge University Press, Cambridge, UK.

Hal Daumé III and Daniel Marcu. 2006. Domain Adaptation for Statistical Classifiers. *Journal of Artificial Intelligence Research*, 26:101–126.

T. Mark Ellison and Simon Kirby. 2006. Measuring Language Divergence by Intra-Lexical Comparison. *Proceedings of the 21st International Conference on Computational Linguistics and 44th Annual Meeting of the ACL*, 273–280. Association for Computational Linguistics. Sidney, Australia.

Jesús Giménez and Lluís Márquez. 2004. SVMTool: A general POS tagger generator based on Support Vector Machines. *Proceedings of the 4th International Conference on Language Resources and Evaluation (LREC'04)*, 43–46. European Language Resources Association. Lisbon, Portugal.

Daniel Kifer, Shai Ben-David, and Johannes Gehrke. 2004. Detecting change in data streams. *Proceedings of the 30th Very Large Data Bases Conference (VLDB'04)*, 180–191. VLDB Endowment. Toronto, Canada.

Solomon Kullback and Richard. A. Leibler. 1951. On Information and Sufficiency. *The Annals of Mathematical Statistics*, 22(1):79–86.

Lillian Lee. 2001. On the Effectiveness of the Skew Divergence for Statistical Language Analysis. *8th International Workshop on Artificial Intelligence and Statistics (AISTATS 2001)*, 65–72. Florida, USA. Online repository http://www.gatsby.ucl.ac.uk/aistats/aistats2001 (Last accessed: April 2, 2010).

Geoffrey Leech, Roger Garside, and Michael Bryant. 1994. CLAWS4: The tagging of the British National Corpus. *Proceedings of the 15th International Conference on Computational Linguistics (COLING 94)*, 622–628. Kyoto, Japan.

Michael Pacey, Steven Fligelstone, and Paul Rayson. 1997. How to generalize the task of annotation. *Corpus Annotation: Linguistic Information from Computer Text Corpora*, 122–136. London: Longman.

Alfréd Rényi. 1961. On measures of information and entropy. *Proceedings of the 4th Berkeley Symposium on Mathematics, Statistics and Probability*, 1:547–561. University of California Press. Berkeley, California, USA.

Self-Training without Reranking for Parser Domain Adaptation and Its Impact on Semantic Role Labeling

Kenji Sagae
Institute for Creative Technologies
University of Southern California
Marina del Rey, CA 90292
sagae@ict.usc.edu

Abstract

We compare self-training with and without reranking for parser domain adaptation, and examine the impact of syntactic parser adaptation on a semantic role labeling system. Although self-training without reranking has been found not to improve in-domain accuracy for parsers trained on the WSJ Penn Treebank, we show that it is surprisingly effective for parser domain adaptation. We also show that simple self-training of a syntactic parser improves out-of-domain accuracy of a semantic role labeler.

1 Introduction

Improvements in data-driven parsing approaches, coupled with the development of treebanks that serve as training data, have resulted in accurate parsers for several languages. However, portability across domains remains a challenge: parsers trained using a treebank for a specific domain generally perform comparatively poorly in other domains. In English, the most widely used training set for parsers comes from the Wall Street Journal portion of the Penn Treebank (Marcus et al., 1993), and constituent parsers trained on this set are now capable of labeled bracketing precision and recall of over 90% (Charniak and Johnson, 2005; Huang, 2008) on WSJ testing sentences. When applied without adaptation to the Brown portion of the Penn Treebank, however, an absolute drop of over 5% in precision and recall is typically observed (McClosky et al., 2006b). In pipelined NLP applications that include a parser, this drop often results in severely degraded results downstream.

We present experiments with a simple self-training approach to semi-supervised parser domain adaptation that produce results that contradict the commonly held assumption that improved parser accuracy cannot be obtained by self-training a generative parser without reranking (Charniak, 1997; Steedman et al., 2003; McClosky et al., 2006b, 2008).[1] We compare this simple self-training approach to the self-training with reranking approach proposed by McClosky et al. (2006b), and show that although McClosky et al.'s approach produces better labeled bracketing precision and recall on out-of-domain sentences, higher F-score on syntactic parses may not lead to an overall improvement in results obtained in NLP applications that include parsing, contrary to our expectations. This is evidenced by results obtained when different adaptation approaches are applied to a parser that serves as a component in a semantic role labeling (SRL) system. This is, to our knowledge, the first attempt to quantify the benefits of semi-supervised parser domain adaptation in semantic role labeling, a task in which parsing accuracy is crucial.

2 Semi-supervised parser domain adaptation with self-training

Because treebanks are expensive to create, while plain text in most domains is easily obtainable, semi-supervised approaches to parser domain adaptation are a particularly attractive solution to the domain portability problem. This usually involves a manually annotated training set (a

[1] Reichart and Rappoport (2007) show that self-training without reranking is effective when the manually annotated training set is small. We show that this is true even for a large training set (the standard WSJ Penn Treebank training set, with over 40k sentences).

Proceedings of the 2010 Workshop on Domain Adaptation for Natural Language Processing, ACL 2010, pages 37–44,
Uppsala, Sweden, 15 July 2010.

treebank), and a larger set of unlabeled data (plain text).

Bacchiani and Roark (2003) obtained positive results in unsupervised domain adaptation of language models by using a speech recognition system with an out-of-domain language model to produce an automatically annotated training corpus that is used to adapt the language model using a maximum *a posteriori* (MAP) adaptation strategy. In subsequent work (Roark and Bacchiani, 2003), this MAP adaptation approach was applied to PCFG adaptation, where an out-of-domain parser was used to annotate an in-domain corpus automatically with multiple candidate trees per sentence. A substantial improvement was achieved in out-of-domain parsing, although the obtained accuracy level was still far below that obtained with domain-specific training data.

More recent work in unsupervised domain adaptation for state-of-the-art parsers has achieved accuracy levels on out-of-domain text that is comparable to that achieved with domain-specific training data (McClosky et al., 2006b). This is done in a self-training setting, where a parser trained on a treebank (in a seed domain) is used to parse a large amount of unlabeled data in the target domain (assigning only one parse per sentence). The automatically parsed corpus is then used as additional training data for the parser. Although initial attempts to improve in-domain parsing accuracy with self-training were unsuccessful (Charniak, 1997; Steedman et al., 2003), recent work has shown that self-training can work in specific conditions (McClosky et al., 2006b), and in particular it can be used to improve parsing accuracy on out-of-domain text (Reichart and Rappoport, 2007).

2.1 Self-training with reraking

McClosky et al. (2006b) presented the most successful semi-supervised approach to date for adaptation of a WSJ-trained parser to Brown data containing several genres of text (such as religion, mystery, romance, adventure, etc.), obtaining a substantial accuracy improvement using only unlabeled data. Their approach involves the use of a first-stage n-best parser and a reranker, which together produce parses for the unlabeled dataset. The automatically parsed in-domain corpus is then used as additional training material. In light of previous failed attempts to improve generative parsers through self-training (Charniak, 1997; Steedman et al., 2003), McClosky et al. (2006a) argue that the use of a reranker is an important factor in the success of their approach. That work used text from the LA Times (taken from the North American News Corpus, or NANC), which is presumably more similar to the parser's training material than to text in the Brown corpus, and resulted not only in an improvement of parser accuracy on out-of-domain text (from the Brown corpus), but also in an improvement in accuracy on in-domain text (the standard WSJ test set of the Penn Treebank).

It can be argued that the McClosky et al. approach is not a pure instance of self-training, since two parsing models are used: the first-stage generative model, and a discriminative model for reranking. The generative parser is improved based on the output of the discriminative model, but McClosky et al. found that the discriminative model does not improve when retrained with its own output.

2.2 Self-training without reraking

Although there have been instances of self-training (or similar) approaches that produced improved parser accuracy without reranking, the success of these efforts are often attributed to other specific factors.

Reichart and Rappoport (2007) obtained positive results in in-domain and out-of-domain scenarios with self-training without reranking, but under the constant condition that only a relatively small set of manually labeled data is used as the seed training set. Sagae and Tsujii (2007) improved the out-of-domain accuracy of a dependency parser trained on the entire WSJ training set (40k sentences) by using unlabeled data in the same domain as the out-of-domain test data (biomedical text). However, they used agreement between different parsers to estimate the quality of automatically generated training instances and selected only sentences with high estimated accuracy. Although the parser improves when trained with its own output, the training instances are selected through the use of a separate dependency parsing model.

2.3 Simple self-training without reranking for domain adaptation

It is now commonly assumed that the simplest form of self-training, where a single parsing model is retrained with its own output (a single parse tree per sentence, without reranking or other means of training instance selection or estimation of parse quality), does not improve the model's accuracy.[2] This assumption, however, is largely based on previous attempts to improve *in-domain* accuracy through self-training (Steedman et al., 2003; Charniak, 1997; McClosky et al., 2006a, 2008). We will refer to this type of self-training as *simple self-training*, to avoid confusion with other self-training settings, such as McClosky et al.'s, where a reranker is involved.

We propose a simple self-training framework for domain adaptation, as follows:

1. A generative parser is trained using a treebank in a specific source domain.

2. The parser is used to generate parse trees from text in a target domain, different from the source domain.

3. The parser is retrained using the original treebank, augmented with the parse trees generated in step 2.

There are intuitive reasons that may lead one to assume that simple self-training *should not* work. One is that no additional information is provided to the model. In self-training with reranking, the generative model can be enriched with information produced by the discriminative model. When two parsers are used for training instance selection, one parser informs the other. In simple self-training, however, there is no additional source of syntactic knowledge with which the self-trained model would be enriched.

Another possible reason is that the output of the self-trained parser should be expected to include the same errors found in the automatically generated training material. If the initial parser has poor accuracy on the target domain, the training data it generates will be of poor quality, resulting in no improvement in the resulting trained model. The self-trained model may simply learn to make the same mistakes as the original model.

Conversely, there are also intuitive reasons for why it *might* work. A possible source of poor performance in new domains is that the model lacks coverage. Specific lexical items and syntactic structures in a new domain appear in a variety of contexts, accompanied by different words and structures. The parser trained on the source domain may analyze some of these new items and structures correctly, and it may also make mistakes. As long as errors in the automatically generated training material are not all systematic, the benefits of adding target-domain information could outweigh the addition of noise in the model.

Naturally, it may be that these conditions hold for some pairs of source and target domains but not others. In the next section, we present experiments that investigate whether simple self-training is effective for one particular set of training (WSJ) and testing (Brown) corpora, which are widely used in parsing research for English.

3 Domain adaptations experiments

In our experiments we use primarily the Charniak (2000) parser. In a few specific experiments we also use the Charniak and Johnson (2005) reranker; such cases are noted explicitly and are not central to the paper, serving mostly for comparisons. We follow the three steps described in section 2.3. The manually labeled training corpus is the standard WSJ training sections of the Penn Treebank (sections 02 to 21). Sections 22 and 23 are used as in-domain development and testing sets, respectively. The out-of-domain material is taken from the Brown portion of the Penn Treebank. We use the same Brown test set as McClosky et al. (2006b), every tenth sentence in the corpus. Another tenth of the corpus is used as a development set, and the rest of the Brown corpus is not used. The out-of-domain text then contains not one but several genres of text. The larger set of unlabeled data is composed of approximately 5.3 million words (320k sentences) of 20th century novels available from Project Gutenberg[3], which do not match exactly the target domain, but is closer to it in general than to the source domain (WSJ).

3.1 Simple self-training results

The precision, recall and F-score of labeled brackets of the initial parser, trained only on the WSJ Penn Treebank, are shown in the first row of results in Table 1 for the WSJ (in-domain) test set and the Brown (out-of-domain) test set. These figures serve as our baseline. The second row of results in Table 1 shows the results obtained with a model produced using simple self-training. The baseline model is used to parse the entire unlabeled dataset (320k sentences), and

[2] Except for in cases where the initial model is trained using a very small treebank.

[3] http://www.gutenberg.org

	WSJ			Brown		
	Precision	Recall	F-score	Precision	Recall	F-score
Baseline	89.49	88.78	89.13	83.93	83.19	83.56
Self-trained	88.26	87.86	88.06	**85.78**	**85.05**	**85.42**
MCJ			91.0			87.1

Table 1. Labeled constituent precision, recall and F-score for the WSJ and Brown test sets, obtained with the baseline model (trained only on the WSJ training set) and with the self-trained model. Results on Brown show an absolute improvement of almost 2%, while results on WSJ show a drop of about 1%. The last row shows the results obtained by McClosky et al. (2006a, 2006b) using self-training with reranking (denoted as MCJ), for comparison purposes.

the resulting parse trees are added to the WSJ training set to produce the self-trained model.

A substantial improvement is observed for the target test set (Brown), close to an absolute improvement of 2% in precision, recall and F-score. Table 1 also shows that parser accuracy fell by 1% on WSJ. Although we do not see this as a problem, since the our goal is to produce an improved model for parsing Brown, it is interesting that, unlike in the work of McClosky et al. (2006a, 2006b) where self-training includes reranking, simple self-training is effective specifically for domain adaptation, but not for improving the accuracy of the parser on in-domain data. At least in this case, simple self-training does not result in an absolutely improved parsing model (as appears to be the case with McClosky et al.'s self-training), although it *does* result in an improved model for the target data.

Finally, the last row in Table 1 shows the results on WSJ and Brown obtained by McClosky et al. (2006a, 2006b) using self-training with reranking. As they have shown, the discriminative reranker can be used to provide further improvements, as discussed in the next subsection.

Unlike McClosky et al. (2006a), we did not give different weights to the original and automatically generated training instances. In our experiments with the Brown development data, varying the weight of the gold-standard WSJ training data from 1 to 7, we observed only small differences in F-score (Table 2). The highest F-score, obtained when the WSJ training corpus is given a relative weight of 3, was only 0.07 higher than the F-score obtained when the WSJ training corpus is given a relative weight of 1.

WSJ relative weight	Brown dev F-score
1	84.51
2	84.52
3	84.58
4	84.53
5	84.51
6	84.55
7	84.57
Baseline (WSJ only)	82.91

Table 2: Brown development set F-scores obtained with self-trained models with different relative weights given to the gold-standard WSJ training data. The last row shows the F-score for the original model (without adaptation).

Table 3 shows results on the Brown development set when different amounts of unlabeled data are used to create the self-trained model. Although F-score generally increases with more unlabeled data, the effect is not monotonic. McClosky et al. observed a similar effect in their self-training experiments, and hypothesized that this may be due to differences between portions of the unlabeled data and the target corpus, and to varying parsing difficulty in portions of the unlabeled data, which results in varying quality of the parse trees produced automatically for training. A large improvement in F-score over the baseline is observed when adding only 30k sentences. Additional improvement is observed when additional sentences are added, but these are small in comparison. One interesting note is

Sentences added	Brown dev. F-score
0 (baseline)	82.91
10k	83.76
20k	84.02
30k	84.29
50k	84.26
100k	84.19
150k	84.38
200k	84.51
250k	84.42
300k	84.51

Table 3: Brown development set F-scores obtained with self-trained models created with different amounts of unlabeled data.

that, although self-training produced improved bracketing precision and recall, part-of-speech tagging accuracy of Brown remained largely unchanged from the baseline, in the range of 94.42% to 94.50% accuracy. It is possible that separate adaption for part-of-speech tagging may improve parsing F-score further.

The results in this section show that simple self-training is effective in adapting WSJ-trained parser to Brown, but more experiments are needed to determine if the same effects observed in our simple self-training experiments would also be observed with other pairs of seed training data and target datasets, and what characteristics of the datasets may affect domain adaptation.

3.2 Self-training with reranking results

To provide a more informative comparison between the results obtained with simple self-training and other work, we also performed McClosky et al.'s self-training with reranking using our unlabeled dataset. In this experiment, intended to provide a better understanding of the role of the unlabeled data (20th century novels vs. LA Times articles), we parse the unlabeled dataset with the Charniak (2000) parser and the Charniak and Johnson (2005) discriminative reranker to produce additional training material for the generative parser. The resulting generative parser produces slightly improved F-scores compared to the simple self-training setting (88.78% on WSJ and 86.01 on Brown), although a slight drop in WSJ F-score is still observed, indicating that the use of news text is likely an important factor in McClosky et al.'s superior F-score figures.

All of these models can be used to produce n-best parses with the Charniak parser, and these can be reranked with the Charniak and Johnson reranker, whether or not the self-training procedure that created the generative model involved reranking. McClosky et al. found that although their self-training procedure involves reranking, the gains in accuracy are orthogonal to those provided by a final reranking step, applied to the output of the self-trained model. As in their case, applying the WSJ-trained reranker to our self-trained model improves its accuracy. In the case of our simple self-trained model, the improvement is of about 1.7%, which means that if a reranker is used at run-time (but not during self-training), F-score goes up to 87.12%. Interestingly, applying a final pass of reranking to the model obtained with self-training with reranking brings F-score up only by less than 1.2%, to 87.17%. So at least in our case, improvements provided by the use the reranker appear not to be completely orthogonal.

4 Semantic Role Labeling with syntactic parser adaptation

To investigate the impact of parser domain adaptation through self-training on applications that depend on parser output, we use an existing semantic role labeling (SRL) system, the Illinois Semantic Role Labeler[4], replacing the provided parsing component with our (WSJ) baseline and (adapted) self-trained parsers.

We tested the SRL system using the datasets of the CoNLL 2005 shared task (Carreras and Màrquez, 2005). The system is trained on the WSJ domain using PropBank (Palmer et al. 2005), and the shared task includes WSJ and Brown evaluation sets. Using the baseline WSJ syntactic parser, the SRL system has an F-score of 77.49 on WSJ, which is a competitive result for systems using a single syntactic analysis per sentence. The highest scoring system (also a UIUC system) in the shared task has 79.44 F-score, and used multiple parse trees, which has been shown to improve results (Punyakanok et al., 2005). On the Brown evaluation, F-score is 64.75, a steep drop from the performance of the system on WSJ, which reflects that not just the syntactic parser, but also other system components, were trained with WSJ material. The

[4] http://l2r.cs.uiuc.edu/~cogcomp/asoftware.php?skey=SRL

	Precision	Recall	F-score
Baseline (WSJ parser)	66.57	63.02	64.75
Simple self-trained parser (this paper)	**71.66**	**66.10**	**68.77**
MCJ self-trained parser	69.18	65.37	67.22
MCJ self-train and rerank	68.62	65.78	67.17

Table 4. Semantic role labeling results using the Illinois Semantic Role Labeler (trained on WSJ material from PropBank) using four different parsing models: (1) a model trained on WSJ, (2) a model built from the WSJ training data and 320k sentences from novels as unlabeled data, using the simple self-training procedure described in sections 2.3 and 3.1, (3) the McClosky et al. (2006a) self-trained model, and (4) the McClosky et al. self-trained model, reranked with the Charniak and Johnson (2005) reranker.

highest scoring system on the Brown evaluation in the CoNLL 2005 shared task had 67.75 F-score.

Table 4 shows the results on the Brown evaluation set using the baseline WSJ SRL system and the results obtained under three self-training parser domain adaptation schemes: simple self-training using novels as unlabeled data (section 3.1), the self-trained model of McClosky et al.[5], and the reranked results of the McClosky et al. self-trained model (which has F-score comparable to that of a parser trained on the Brown corpus).

As expected, the contributions of the three adapted parsing models allowed the system to produce overall SRL results that are better than those produced with the baseline setting. Surprisingly, however, the use of the model created using simple self-training and sentences from novels (sections 2.3 and 3.1) resulted in better SRL results than the use of McClosky et al.'s reranking-based self-trained model (whether its results go through one additional step of reranking or not), which produces substantially higher syntactic parsing F-score. Our self-trained parsing model results in an absolute increase of 4% in SRL F-score, outscoring all participants in the shared task (of course, systems in the shared task did not use adapted parsing models or external resources, such as unlabeled data). The improvement in the precision of the SRL system using simple self-training is particularly large. Improvements in the precision of the core arguments Arg0, Arg1, Arg2 contributed heavily to the improvement of overall scores.

We note that other parts of the SRL system remained constant, and the difference in the results shown in Table 4 come solely from the use of different (adapted) parsers.

5 Conclusion

We explored the use of simple self-training, where no reranking or confidence measurements are used, for parser domain adaptation. We found that self-training can in fact improve the accuracy of a parser in a different domain from the domain of its training data (even when the training data is the entire standard WSJ training material from the Penn Treebank), and that this improvement can be carried on to modules that may use the output of the parser. We demonstrated that a semantic role labeling system trained with WSJ training data can improve substantially (4%) on Brown just by having its parser be adapted using unlabeled data.

Although the fact that self-training produces improved parsing results without reranking does not necessarily conflict with previous work, it does contradict the widely held assumption that this type of self-training does not improve parser accuracy. One way to reconcile expectations based on previous attempts to improve parsing accuracy with self-training (Charniak, 1997;

[5] http://www.cs.brown.edu/~dmcc/selftraining.html

Steedman et al., 2003) and the results observed in our experiments is that we focus specifically on domain adaptation. In fact, the in-domain accuracy of our adapted model is slightly inferior to that of the baseline, more in line with previous findings.

This work represents only one additional step towards understanding of how and when self-training works for parsing and for domain adaptation. Additional analysis and experiments are needed to understand under what conditions and in what domains simple self-training can be effective.

One question that seems particularly interesting is why the models adapted using self-training with reranking and news text, which produce substantially higher parsing F-scores, did not outperform our model built with simple self-training in contribution to the SRL system. Although we do not have an answer to this question, two factors that may play a role are the domain of the training data and the use of the reranker, which may provide improvements in parse quality that are of a different kind of those most needed by the SRL system. This points to another interesting direction, where adapted parsers can be combined. Having different ways to perform semi-supervised parser adaptation may result in the creation of adapted models with improved accuracy on a target domain but different characteristics. The output of these parsers could then be combined in a voting scheme (Henderson and Brill, 1999) for additional improvements on the target domain.

Acknowledgments

We thank Andrew S. Gordon and the anonymous reviewers for valuable comments and suggestions. The work described here has been sponsored by the U.S. Army Research, Development, and Engineering Command (RDECOM). Statements and opinions expressed do not necessarily reflect the position or the policy of the United States Government, and no official endorsement should be inferred.

References

Michiel Bacchiani and Brian Roark. 2003. Unsupervised language model adaptation. In *Proceedings of the International Conference on Acoustics, Speech and Signal Processing (ICASSP).*

Xavier Carreras and Lluís Màrquez. 2005. Introduction to the CoNLL-2005 Shared Task: Semantic Role Labeling. In *Proceedings of the CoNLL 2005 shared task.*

Eugene Charniak. 1997. Statistical parsing with a context-free grammar and word statistics. In *Proceedings of AAAI*, pages 598–603.

Eugene Charniak. 2000. A maximum-entropy-inspired parser. In *Proceedings of the First Meeting of the North American Chapter of the Association for Computational Linguistics (NAACL).* Pages 132-139. Seattle, WA.

Eugene Charniak and Mark Johnson. 2005. Coarse-to-fine n-best parsing and MaxEnt discriminative reranking. In *Proceedings of the 2005 Meeting of the Association for Computational Linguistics (ACL)*, pages 173–180.

John C. Henderson, Eric Brill. 1999. Exploiting Diversity in Natural Language Processing: Combining Parsers. In *Proceedings of the Fourth Conference on Empirical Methods in Natural Language Processing (EMNLP-99),* pp. 187–194. College Park, Maryland.

Liang Huang (2008). Forest Reranking: Discriminative Parsing with Non-Local Features. In *Proceedings of the 2008 Meeting of the Association for Computational Linguistics (ACL).* Columbus, OH.

Mitchell P. Marcus, Mary Ann Marcinkiewicz and Beatrice Santorini. 1993. Building a large annotated corpus of English: the Penn Treebank. In *Computational Linguistics 19*(2), 313-330.

David McClosky, Eugene Charniak and Mark Johnson. 2006a. Effective self-training for parsing. In *Proceedings of the Main Conference on Human Language Technology Conference of the North American Chapter of the Association of Computational Linguistics (NAACL).* New York, NY.

David McClosky, Eugene Charniak and Mark Johnson. 2006b. Reranking and self-training for parser adaptation. In *Proceedings of the 21st international Conference on Computational Linguistics and the 44th Annual Meeting of the Association For Computational Linguistics (ACL).* Sydney, Australia.

David McClosky, Eugene Charniak and Mark Johnson. 2008. When is self-training effective for parsing? In *Proceedings of the 22nd international Conference on Computational Linguistics (COLING) - Volume 1.* Manchester, United Kingdom.

Martha Palmer, Daniel Gildea, and Paul Kingsbury. 2005. The proposition bank: An annotated corpus of semantic roles. *Computational Linguistics*, 31(1).

Vasin Punyakanok, Peter Koomen, Dan Roth and Wen-tau Yih. 2005. Generalized Inference with Multiple Semantic Role Labeling Systems. In *Proceedings of the CoNLL 2005 shared task.*

Roi Reichart and Ari Rappoport. 2007. Self-training for enhancement and domain adaptation of statistical parsers trained on small datasets. In *Proceedings of the 45th Annual Meeting of the Association for Computational Linguistics (ACL)*. Pages 616-623. Prague, Czech Republic.

Brian Roark and Michiel Bacchiani. 2003. Supervised and unsupervised PCFG adaptation to novel domains. In *Proceedings of the 2003 Conference of the North American Chapter of the Association for Computational Linguistics on Human Language Technology – Volume 1 (NAACL-HLT)*.

Kenji Sagae and Jun'ichi Tsujii. 2007. Multilingual dependency parsing and domain adaptation with data-driven LR models and parser ensembles. In *Proceedings of the CoNLL 2007 shared task*. Prague, Czech Republic.

Mark Steedman, Rebecca Hwa, Stephen Clark, Miles Osborne, Anoop Sarkar, Julia Hockenmaier, Paul Ruhlen, Steven Baker and Jeremiah Crim. 2003. Bootstrapping statistical parsers from small datasets. In *Proceedings of Tenth Conference of the European Chapter of the Association for Computational Linguistics (EACL) – Volume 1*. Budapest, Hungary.

Domain Adaptation with Unlabeled Data for Dialog Act Tagging

Anna Margolis[1,2] **Karen Livescu**[2] **Mari Ostendorf**[1]
[1]Department of Electrical Engineering, University of Washington, Seattle, WA, USA.
[2]TTI-Chicago, Chicago, IL, USA.
amargoli@ee.washington.edu, klivescu@ttic.edu, mo@ee.washington.edu

Abstract

We investigate the classification of utterances into high-level dialog act categories using word-based features, under conditions where the train and test data differ by genre and/or language. We handle the cross-language cases with machine translation of the test utterances. We analyze and compare two feature-based approaches to using unlabeled data in adaptation: restriction to a shared feature set, and an implementation of Blitzer et al.'s Structural Correspondence Learning. Both methods lead to increased detection of backchannels in the cross-language cases by utilizing correlations between backchannel words and utterance length.

1 Introduction

Dialog act (or speech act) tagging aims to label abstract functions of utterances in conversations, such as Request, Floorgrab, or Statement; potential applications include automatic conversation analysis, punctuation transcription, and human-computer dialog systems. Although some applications require domain-specific tag sets, it is often useful to label utterances based on generic tags, and several tag sets have been developed for this purpose, e.g. DAMSL (Core and Allen, 1997). Many approaches to automatic dialog act (DA) tagging assume hand-labeled training data. However, when building a new system it may be difficult to find a labeled corpus that matches the target domain, or even the language. Even within the same language, speech from different domains can differ linguistically, and the same DA categories might be characterized by different cues. The domain characteristics (face-to-face vs. telephone, two-party vs. multi-party, informal vs. agenda-driven, familiar vs. stranger) can influence both the distribution of tags and word choice.

This work attempts to use unlabeled target domain data in order to improve cross-domain training performance, an approach referred to as both unsupervised and semi-supervised domain adaptation in the literature. We refer to the labeled training domain as the source domain. We compare two adaptation approaches: a simple one based on forcing the classifier to learn only on "shared" features that appear in both domains, and a more complex one based on Structural Correspondence Learning (SCL) from Blitzer et al. (2007). The shared feature approach has been investigated for adaptation in other tasks, e.g. Aue and Gamon (2005) for sentiment classification and Dredze et al. (2007) for parsing. SCL has been used successfully for sentiment classification and part-of-speech tagging (Blitzer et al., 2006); here we investigate its applicability to the DA classification task, using a multi-view learning implementation as suggested by Blitzer et al. (2009). In addition to analyzing these two methods on a novel task, we show an interesting comparison between them: in this setting, both methods turn out to have a similar effect caused by correlating cues for a particular DA class (Backchannel) with length.

We classify pre-segmented utterances based on their transcripts, and we consider only four high-level classes: Statement, Question, Backchannel, and Incomplete. Experiments are performed using all train/test pairs among three conversational speech corpora : the Meeting Recorder Dialog Act corpus (MRDA) (Shriberg et al., 2004), Switchboard DAMSL (Swbd) (Jurafsky et al., 1997), and the Spanish Callhome dialog act corpus (SpCH) (Levin et al., 1998). The first is multi-party, face-to-face meeting speech; the second is topic-prompted telephone speech between strangers; and the third is informal telephone speech between friends and family members. The first two are in English, while the third is in Spanish. When the source and target domains differ in language, we

Proceedings of the 2010 Workshop on Domain Adaptation for Natural Language Processing, ACL 2010, pages 45–52,
Uppsala, Sweden, 15 July 2010.

apply machine translation to the target domain to convert it to the language of the source domain.

2 Related Work

Automatic DA tagging across domain has been investigated by a handful of researchers. Webb and Liu (2008) investigated cross-corpus training between Swbd and another corpus consisting of task-oriented calls, although no adaptation was attempted. Similarly, Rosset et al. (2008) reported on recognition of task-oriented DA tags across domain and language (French to English) by using utterances that had been pre-processed to extract entities. Tur (2005) applied supervised model adaptation to intent classification across customer dialog systems, and Guz et al. (2010) applied supervised model adaptation methods for DA segmentation and classification on MRDA using labeled data from both MRDA and Swbd. Most similar to our work is that of Jeong et al. (2009), who compared two methods for semi-supervised adaptation, using Swbd/MRDA as the source training set and email or forums corpora as the target domains. Both methods were based on incorporating unlabeled target domain examples into training. Success has also been reported for self-training approaches on same-domain semi-supervised learning (Venkataraman et al., 2003; Tur et al., 2005). We are not aware of prior work on cross-lingual DA tagging via machine translation, although a translation approach has been employed for cross-lingual text classification and information retrieval, e.g. Bel et al. (2003).

In recent years there has been increasing interest in domain adaptation methods based on unlabeled target domain data. Several kinds of approaches have been proposed, including self-training (Roark and Bacchiani, 2003), instance weighting (Huang et al., 2007), change of feature representation (Pan et al., 2008), and clustering methods (Xing et al., 2007). SCL (Blitzer et al., 2006) is one feature representation approach that has been effective on certain high-dimensional NLP problems, including part-of-speech tagging and sentiment classification. SCL uses unlabeled data to learn feature projections that tie together source and target features via their correlations with features shared between domains. It first selects "pivot features" that are common in both domains; next, linear predictors for those features are learned on all the other features. Finally, singular value decomposition (SVD) is performed on the collection of learned linear predictors corresponding to different pivot features. Features that tend to get similar weights in predicting pivot features will be tied together in the SVD. By learning on the SVD dimensions, the source-trained classifier can put weight on target-only features.

3 Methods

Our four-class DA problem is similar to problems studied in other work, such as Tur et al. (2007) who used five classes (ours plus Floorgrab/hold). When defining a mapping from each corpus' tag set to the four high-level classes, our goal was to try to make the classes similarly defined across corpora. Note that the Incomplete category is defined in Swbd-DAMSL to include only utterances too short to determine their DA label (e.g., just a filler word). Thus, for our work the MRDA Incomplete category excludes utterances also tagged as Statement or Question; it includes those consisting of just a floor-grab, hold or filler word.

For classification we used an SVM with linear kernel, with L2 regularization and L1 loss, as implemented in the Liblinear package (Fan et al., 2008) which uses the one-vs.-rest configuration for multiclass classification. SVMs have been successful for supervised learning of DAs based on words and other features (Surendran and Levow, 2006; Liu, 2006). Features are derived from the hand transcripts, which are hand-segmented into DA units. Punctuation and capitalization are removed so that our setting corresponds to classification based on (perfect) speech recognition output. The features are counts of unigrams, bigrams, and trigrams that occur at least twice in the train set, including beginning/end-of-utterance tags ($\langle s \rangle$, $\langle /s \rangle$), and a length feature (total number of words, z-normalized across the training set). Note that some previous work on DA tagging has used contextual features from surrounding utterances, or Markov models for the DA sequence. In addition, some work has used prosodic or other acoustic features. The work of Stolcke et al. (2000) found benefits to using Markov sequence models and prosodic features in addition to word features, but those benefits were relatively small, so for simplicity our experiments here use only word features and classify utterances in isolation.

We used Google Translate to derive English

translations of the Spanish SpCH utterances, and to derive Spanish translations of the English Swbd and MRDA utterances. Of course, translations are far from perfect; DA classification performance could likely be improved by using a translation system trained on spoken dialog. For instance, Google Translate often failed on certain words like "i" that are usually capitalized in text. Even so, when training and testing on translated utterances, the results with the generic system are surprisingly good.

The results reported below used the standard train/test splits provided with the corpora: MRDA had 51 train meetings/11 test; Swbd had 1115 train conversations/19 test; SpCH had 80 train conversations/20 test. The SpCH train set is the smallest at 29k utterances. To avoid issues of differing train set size when comparing performance of different models, we reduced the Swbd and MRDA train sets to the same size as SpCH using randomly selected examples from the full train sets. For each adaptation experiment, we used the target domain training set as the unlabeled data, and report performance on the target domain test set. The test sets contain 4525, 15180, and 3715 utterances for Swbd, MRDA, and SpCH respectively.

4 Results

Table 1 shows the class proportions in the training sets for each domain. MRDA has fewer Backchannels than the the others, which is expected since the meetings are face-to-face. SpCH has fewer Incompletes and more Questions than the others; the reasons for this are unclear. Backchannels have the shortest mean length (less than 2 words) in all domains. Incompletes are also short, while Statements have the longest mean length. The mean lengths of Statements and Questions are similar in the English corpora, but are shorter in SpCH. (This may point to differences in how the utterances were segmented; for instance Swbd utterances can span multiple turns, although 90% are only one turn long.)

Because of the high class skew, we consider two different schemes for training the classifiers, and report different performance measures for each. To optimize overall accuracy, we use basic unweighted training. To optimize average per-class recall (weighted equally across all classes), we use weighted training, where each training example is weighted inversely to its class proportion. We optimize the regularization parameter using a source domain development set corresponding to each training set. Since the optimum values are close for all three domains, we choose a single value for all the accuracy classifiers and a single value for all the per-class recall classifiers. (Different values are chosen for different feature types corresponding to the different adaptation methods.)

	Inc.	Stat.	Quest.	Back.
Swbd	8.1%	67.1%	5.8%	19.1%
MRDA	10.7%	67.9%	7.5%	14.0%
SpCH	5.7%	60.6%	12.1%	21.7%

Table 1: Proportion of utterances in each DA category (Incomplete, Statement, Question, Backchannel) in each domain's training set.

Table 2 gives baseline performance for all train-test pairs, using translated versions of the test set when the train set differs in language. It also lists the in-domain results using translated (train and test) data, and results using the adaptation methods (which we discuss below). Figure 1 shows details of the contribution of each class to the average per-class recall; bar height corresponds to the second column in Table 2.

4.1 Baseline performance and analysis

We observe first that translation does not have a large effect on in-domain performance; degradation occurs primarily in Incompletes and Questions, which depend most on word order and therefore might be most sensitive to ordering differences in the translations. We conclude that it is possible to perform well on the translated test sets when the training data is well matched. However, cross-domain performance degradation is much worse between pairs that differ in language than between the two English corpora.

We now describe three kinds of issues contributing to cross-domain domain degradation, which we observed anecdotally. First, some highly important words in one domain are sometimes missing entirely from another domain. This issue appears to have a dramatic effect on Backchannel detection across languages: when optimizing for average per-class recall, the English-trained classifiers detect about 20% of the Spanish translated Backchannels and the Spanish classifier detects a little over half of the English ones, while they each detect more than 80% in their own domain.

train set	Acc (%)	Avg. Rec. (%)
Test on Swbd		
Swbd	89.2	84.9
Swbd translated	86.7	80.4
MRDA baseline	**86.4**	**78.0**
MRDA shared only	85.7*	77.7
MRDA SCL	81.8*	69.6
MRDA length only	78.3*	51.4
SpCH baseline	74.5	57.2
SpCH shared only	77.4*	64.2
SpCH SCL	76.8*	**64.8**
SpCH length only	**77.7***	48.2
majority	67.7	25.0
Test on MRDA		
MRDA	83.8	80.5
MRDA translated	80.5	74.7
Swbd baseline	**81.0**	71.6
Swbd shared only	80.1*	**72.1**
Swbd SCL	75.6*	68.1
Swbd length only	68.6*	44.9
SpCH baseline	66.9	50.5
SpCH shared only	66.8	52.1
SpCH SCL	66.1*	**58.4**
SpCH length only	**68.3***	44.6
majority	65.2	25.0
Test on SpCH		
SpCH	83.1	72.8
SpCH translated	82.4	71.3
Swbd baseline	63.8	41.1
Swbd shared only	66.2*	**50.9**
Swbd SCL	68.2*	47.2
Swbd length only	**72.6***	43.6
MRDA baseline	65.1	42.9
MRDA shared only	65.5	**51.2**
MRDA SCL	67.6*	50.9
MRDA length only	**72.6***	44.7
majority	65.3	25.0

Table 2: Overall accuracy and average per-class recall on each test set, using in-domain, in-domain translated, and cross-domain training. Starred results under the accuracy column are significantly different from the corresponding cross-domain baseline under McNemar's test ($p < 0.05$). (Significance is not calculated for the average per-class recall column.) "Majority" classifies everything as Statement.

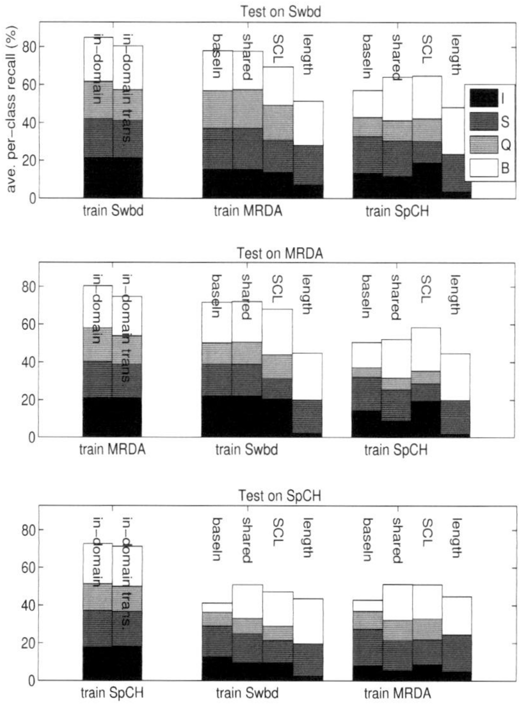

Figure 1: Per-class recall of weighted classifiers in column 2 of Table 2. Bar height represents average per-class recall; colors indicate contribution of each class: I=incomplete, S=statement, Q=question, B=backchannel. (Maximum possible bar height is 100%, each color 25%).

The reason for the cross-domain drop is that many backchannel words in the English corpora (uhhuh, right, yeah) do not overlap with those in the Spanish corpora (mmm, sí, ya) even after translation—for example, "ya" becomes "already", "sí" becomes "yes", "right" becomes "derecho", and "uhhuh", "mmm" are unchanged.

A second issue has to do with different kinds of utterances found in each domain, which sometimes lead to different relationships between features and class label. This is sometimes caused by the translation system; for example, utterances starting with "es que . . ." are usually statements in SpCH, but without capitalization the translator often gives "is that . . .". Since "⟨s⟩–is–that" is a cue feature for Question in English, these utterances are usually labeled as Question by the English domain classifiers. The existence of different types of utterances can result in sets of features that are more highly correlated in one domain than the other. In both Swbd and translated SpCH, utterances containing the trigram "⟨s⟩–but–⟨/s⟩" are most likely to be in the Incomplete class. In Swbd, the bigram "but–⟨/s⟩" rarely occurs outside of that trigram, but in SpCH it sometimes occurs at the end of long (syntactically-incomplete) Statements, so it corresponds to much lower likelihood for the Incomplete class.

The last issue concerns utterances whose true label probabilities given the word sequence are not the same across domains. We distinguish two such kinds utterances. The first are due to class definition differences across domains and annotators, e.g., long statements or questions that are also incomplete are more often labeled Incomplete in SpCH and Swbd than in MRDA. The second kind are utterances whose class labels are not completely determined by their word sequence. To minimize error rate the classifier should label an utterance with its most frequent class, but that may differ across domains. For example, "yes" can be either a Statement of Backchannel; in the English corpora, it is most likely to be a Statement ("yeah" is more commonly used for Backchannels). However, "sí" is most likely to be a Backchannel in SpCH. To measure the effect of differing label probabilities across domains, we trained "domain-general" classifiers using concatenated training sets for each pair of domains. We found that they performed about the same or only slightly worse than domain-specific models, so we conclude that this issue is likely only a minor effect.

4.2 Adaptation using shared features only

In the cross-language domain pairs, some discriminative features in one domain are missing in the other. By removing all features from the source domain training utterances that are not observed (twice) in the target domain training data, we force the classifier to learn only on features that are present in both domains. As seen in Figure 1, this had the effect of improving recall of Backchannels in the four cross-language cases. Backchannels are the second-most frequent class after Statements, and are typically short in all domains. Many typical Backchannel words are domain-specific; by removing them from the source data, we force the classifier to attempt to detect Backchannels based on length alone. The resulting classifier has a better chance of recognizing target domain Backchannels that lack the source-only Backchannel words. At the same time, it mistakes many other short utterances for Backchannels, and does particularly worse on Incompletes, for which length is also strong cue. Although average per-class recall improved in all four cross-language cases, total accuracy only improved significantly in two of those cases, and for the Swbd/MRDA pair, accuracy got significantly worse. The effect on the one-vs.-rest component classifiers was mixed: for some (Statement and some Backchannel classifiers in the cross-language cases), accuracy improved, while in other cases it decreased.

As noted above, the shared feature approach was investigated by Aue and Gamon (2005), who argued that its success depends on the assumption that class/feature relationships be the same across domains. However, we argue here that the success of this method requires stronger assumptions about both the relationship between domains and the correlations between domain-specific and shared features. Consider learning a linear model on either the full source domain feature set or the reduced shared feature set. In general, the coefficients for a given feature will be different in each model—in the reduced case, the coefficients incorporate correlation information and label predictive information for the removed (source-only) features. This is potentially useful on the target domain, provided that there exist analogous, target-only features that have similar correlations with the shared features, and similar predictive coefficients.

For example, consider the discriminative source and target features "uhhuh" and "mmm," which are both are correlated with a shared, noisier, feature (length). Forcing the model to learn only on the shared, noisy feature incorporates correlation information about "uhhuh", which is similar to that of "mmm". Thus, the reduced model is potentially more useful on the target domain, compared to the full source domain model which might not put weight on the noisy feature. On the other hand, the approach is inappropriate in several other scenarios. For one, if the target domain utterances actually represent samples from a subspace of the source domain, the absence of features is informative: the fact that an utterance does not contain "⟨s⟩–verdad–⟨/s⟩", for instance, might mean that it is less likely to be a Question, even if none of the target domain utterances contain this feature.

4.3 Adaptation using SCL

The original formulation of SCL proposed predicting pivot features using the entire feature set, except for those features perfectly correlated with the pivots (e.g., the pivots themselves). Our experiments with this approach found it unsuitable for our task, since even after removing the pivots there are many features which remain highly correlated with the pivots due to overlapping n-grams (i-love vs. love). The number of features that overlap with pivots is large, so removing these would lead to few features being included in the projections. Therefore, we adopted the multi-view learning approach suggested by Blitzer et al. (2009). We split the utterances into two parts; pivot features in the first part were predicted with all the features in the second, and vice versa. We experimented with splitting the utterances in the middle, but found that since the number of words in the first part (nearly) predicts the number in the second part, all of the features in the first part were positively predictive of pivots in the second part so the main dimension learned was length. In the results presented here, the first part consists of the first word only, and the second part is the rest of the utterance. (All utterances in our experiments have at least one word.) Pivot features are selected in each part and predicted using a least-squares linear regression on all features in the other part.

We used the SCL-MI method of Blitzer et al. (2007) to select pivot features, which requires that they be common in both domains and have high mutual information (MI) with the class (according to the source labels.) We selected features that occurred at least 10 times in each domain and were in the top 500 ranked MI features for any of the four classes; this resulted in 78-99 first-part pivots and 787-910 second-part pivots (depending on the source-target pair). We performed SVD on the learned prediction weights for each part separately, and the top (at most) 100 dimensions were used to project utterances on each side.

In all train-test pairs, the first dimension of the first part appeared to distinguish short utterance words from long ones. Such short-utterance words included backchannels from both domains, in addition to acknowledgments, exclamations, swear words and greetings. An analogous dimension existed in the second part, which captured words correlated with short utterances greater than one word (right, really, interesting). The other dimensions of both domains were difficult to interpret.

We experimented with using the SCL features together with the raw features (n-grams and length), as suggested by (Blitzer et al., 2006). As in (Blitzer et al., 2006), we found it necessary to scale up the SCL features to increase their utilization in the presence of the raw features; however, it was difficult to guess the optimal scaling factor without having access to labeled target data. The results here use SCL features only, which also allows us to more clearly investigate the utility of those features and to compare them with the other feature sets.

The most notable effect was an improvement in Backchannel recall, which occurred under both weighted and unweighted training. In addition, there was high confusability between Statements and the other classes, and more false detections of Backchannels. When optimizing for accuracy, SCL led to an improvement in accuracy in three of the four cross-language cases. When optimizing for average per-class recall, it led to improvement in all cross-language cases; however, recall of Statements went down dramatically in all cases. In addition, while there was no clear benefit of the SCL vs. the shared-feature method on the cross-language cases, the SCL approach did much worse than the shared-feature approach on the Swbd/MRDA pair, causing large degradation from the baseline.

As we have noted, utterance length appears to underlie the improvement seen in the cross-language performance for both the SCL and shared-feature approaches. Therefore, we include results for a classifier based only on the length feature. Optimizing for accuracy, this method achieves the highest accuracy of all methods in the cross-language pairs. (It does so by classifying everything as Statement or Backchannel, although with weighted training, as shown in Figure 1, it gets some Incompletes.) However, under weighted class training, the average per-class recall of this method is much worse than the shared-feature and SCL approaches.

Comparison with other SCL tasks Although we basically take a text classification approach to the problem of dialog act tagging, our problem differs in several ways from the sentiment classification task in Blitzer et al. (2007). In particular, utterances are much shorter than documents, and we use position information via the start/end-of-sentence tags. Some important DA cue features (such as the value of the first word) are mutually exclusive rather than correlated. In this way our problem resembles the part-of-speech tagging task

(Blitzer et al., 2006), where the category of each word is predicted using values of the left, right, and current word token. In fact, that work used a kind of multi-view learning for the SCL projection, with three views corresponding to the three word categories. However, our problem essentially uses a mix of bag-of-words and position-based features, which poses a greater challenge since there is no natural multi-view split. The approach described here suffers from the fact that it cannot use all the features available to the baseline classifier—bigrams and trigrams spanning the first and second words are left out. It also suffers from the fact that the first-word pivot feature set is extremely small—a consequence of the small set of first words that occur at least 10 times in the 29k-utterance corpora.

5 Conclusions

We have considered two approaches for domain adaptation for DA tagging, and analyzed their performance for source/target pairs drawn from three different domains. For the English domains, the baseline cross-domain performance was quite good, and both adaptation methods generally led to degradation over the baseline. For the cross-language cases, both methods were effective at improving average per-class recall, and particularly Backchannel recall. SCL led to significant accuracy improvement in three cases, while the shared feature approach did so in two cases. On the other hand, SCL showed poor discrimination between Statements and other classes, and did worse on the same-language pair that had little cross-domain degradation. Both methods work by taking advantage of correlations between shared and domain-specific class-discriminative features. Unfortunately in our task, membership in the rare classes is often cued by features that are mutually exclusive, e.g., the starting n-gram for Questions. Both methods might therefore benefit from additional shared features that are correlated with these n-grams, e.g., sentence-final intonation for Questions. (Indeed, other work on semi-supervised DA tagging has used a richer feature set: Jeong et al. (2009) included parse, part-of-speech, and speaker sequence information, and Venkataraman et al. (2003) used prosodic information, plus a sequence-modeling framework.) From the task perspective, an interesting result is that machine translation appears to preserve most of the dialog-act information, in that in-domain performance is similar on original and translated text.

Acknowledgments

We thank Sham Kakade for suggesting the multi-view SCL method based on utterance splits and for many other helpful discussions, as well as John Blitzer for helpful discussions. We thank the three reviewers for their useful comments.

This research was funded by the Office of the Director of National Intelligence (ODNI), Intelligence Advanced Research Projects Activity (IARPA). All statements of fact, opinion or conclusions contained herein are those of the authors and should not be construed as representing the official views or policies of IARPA, the ODNI or the U.S. Government.

References

Anthony Aue and Michael Gamon. 2005. Customizing sentiment classifiers to new domains: a case study. In *Proc. International Conference on Recent Advances in NLP*.

Nuria Bel, Cornelis H. A. Koster, and Marta Villegas. 2003. Cross-lingual text categorization. In *Research and Advanced Technology for Digital Libraries*, pages 126–139. Springer Berlin / Heidelberg.

John Blitzer, Ryan McDonald, and Fernando Pereira. 2006. Domain adaptation with structural correspondence learning. In *Proc. of the 2006 Conference on Empirical Methods in Natural Language Processing*, pages 120–128.

John Blitzer, Mark Dredze, and Fernando Pereira. 2007. Biographies, Bollywood, boom-boxes and blenders: Domain adaptation for sentiment classification. In *Proceedings of the 45th Annual Meeting of the Association of Computational Linguistics*, pages 440–447.

John Blitzer, Dean P. Foster, and Sham M. Kakade. 2009. Zero-shot domain adaptation: A multi-view approach. Technical report, Toyota Technological Institute TTI-TR-2009-1.

Mark G. Core and James F. Allen. 1997. Coding dialogs with the DAMSL annotation scheme. In *Proc. of the Working Notes of the AAAI Fall Symposium on Communicative Action in Humans and Machines*.

Mark Dredze, John Blitzer, Partha Pratim Talukdar, Kuzman Ganchev, João Graca, and Fernando Pereira. 2007. Frustratingly hard domain adaptation for dependency parsing. In *Proc. of the CoNLL Shared Task Session of EMNLP-CoNLL 2007*, pages 1051–1055.

Rong-En Fan, Kai-Wei Chang, Cho-Jui Hsieh, Xiang-Rui Wang, and Chih-Jen Lin. 2008. Liblinear: A library for large linear classification. *Journal of Machine Learning Research*, 9:1871–1874.

Umit Guz, Gokhan Tur, Dilek Hakkani-Tür, and Sébastien Cuendet. 2010. Cascaded model adaptation for dialog act segmentation and tagging. *Computer Speech & Language*, 24(2):289–306.

Jiayuan Huang, Alexander J. Smola, Arthur Gretton, Karsten M. Borgwardt, and Bernhard Schölkopf. 2007. Correcting sample selection bias by unlabeled data. In *Advances in Neural Information Processing Systems 19*, pages 601–608.

Minwoo Jeong, Chin Y. Lin, and Gary G. Lee. 2009. Semi-supervised speech act recognition in emails and forums. In *Proc. of the 2009 Conference on Empirical Methods in Natural Language Processing*, pages 1250–1259.

Dan Jurafsky, Liz Shriberg, and Debra Biasca. 1997. Switchboard SWBD-DAMSL shallow-discourse-function annotation coders manual, draft 13. Technical report, University of Colorado at Boulder Technical Report 97-02.

Lori Levin, Ann Thymé-Gobbel, Alon Lavie, Klaus Ries, and Klaus Zechner. 1998. A discourse coding scheme for conversational Spanish. In *Proc. The 5th International Conference on Spoken Language Processing*, pages 2335–2338.

Yang Liu. 2006. Using SVM and error-correcting codes for multiclass dialog act classification in meeting corpus. In *Proc. Interspeech*, pages 1938–1941.

Sinno J. Pan, James T. Kwok, and Qiang Yang. 2008. Transfer learning via dimensionality reduction. In *Proc. of the Twenty-Third AAAI Conference on Artificial Intelligence*.

Brian Roark and Michiel Bacchiani. 2003. Supervised and unsupervised PCFG adaptation to novel domains. In *Proc. of the 2003 Conference of the North American Chapter of the Association for Computational Linguistics on Human Language Technology*, pages 126–133.

Sophie Rosset, Delphine Tribout, and Lori Lamel. 2008. Multi-level information and automatic dialog act detection in human–human spoken dialogs. *Speech Communication*, 50(1):1–13.

Elizabeth Shriberg, Raj Dhillon, Sonali Bhagat, Jeremy Ang, and Hannah Carvey. 2004. The ICSI meeting recorder dialog act (MRDA) corpus. In *Proc. of the 5th SIGdial Workshop on Discourse and Dialogue*, pages 97–100.

Andreas Stolcke, Klaus Ries, Noah Coccaro, Elizabeth Shriberg, Rebecca Bates, Daniel Jurafsky, Paul Taylor, Rachel Martin, Carol Van Ess-Dykema, and Marie Meteer. 2000. Dialogue act modeling for automatic tagging and recognition of conversational speech. *Computational Linguistics*, 26:339–373.

Dinoj Surendran and Gina-Anne Levow. 2006. Dialog act tagging with support vector machines and hidden Markov models. In *Proc. Interspeech*, pages 1950–1953.

Gokhan Tur, Dilek Hakkani-Tür, and Robert E. Schapire. 2005. Combining active and semi-supervised learning for spoken language understanding. *Speech Communication*, 45(2):171–186.

Gokhan Tur, Umit Guz, and Dilek Hakkani-Tür. 2007. Model adaptation for dialog act tagging. In *Proc. IEEE Spoken Language Technology Workshop*, pages 94–97.

Gokhan Tur. 2005. Model adaptation for spoken language understanding. In *Proc. IEEE International Conference on Acoustics, Speech, and Signal Processing*, pages 41–44.

Anand Venkataraman, Luciana Ferrer, Andreas Stolcke, and Elizabeth Shriberg. 2003. Training a prosody-based dialog act tagger from unlabeled data. In *Proc. IEEE International Conference on Acoustics, Speech, and Signal Processing*, volume I, pages 272–275.

Nick Webb and Ting Liu. 2008. Investigating the portability of corpus-derived cue phrases for dialogue act classification. In *Proc. of the 22nd International Conference on Computational Linguistics (Coling 2008)*, pages 977–984.

Dikan Xing, Wenyuan Dai, Gui-Rong Xue, and Yong Yu. 2007. Bridged refinement for transfer learning. In *Knowledge Discovery in Databases: PKDD 2007*, pages 324–335. Springer Berlin / Heidelberg.

Frustratingly Easy Semi-Supervised Domain Adaptation

Hal Daumé III
School Of Computing
University of Utah
hal@cs.utah.edu

Abhishek Kumar
School Of Computing
University of Utah
abhik@cs.utah.edu

Avishek Saha
School Of Computing
University of Utah
avishek@cs.utah.edu

Abstract

In this work, we propose a semi-supervised extension to a well-known supervised domain adaptation approach (EA) (Daumé III, 2007). Our proposed approach (EA++) builds on the notion of augmented space (introduced in EA) and harnesses unlabeled data in target domain to ameliorate the transfer of information from *source* to *target*. This semi-supervised approach to domain adaptation is extremely simple to implement, and can be applied as a pre-processing step to any supervised learner. Experimental results on sequential labeling tasks demonstrate the efficacy of the proposed method.

1 Introduction

A domain adaptation approach for sequential labeling tasks in NLP was proposed in (Daumé III, 2007). The proposed approach, termed EASYADAPT (EA), augments the *source domain* feature space using features from labeled data in *target domain*. EA is simple, easy to extend and implement as a preprocessing step and most importantly is agnostic of the underlying classifier. However, EA requires labeled data in the target and hence applies to *fully supervised* (labeled data in *source* and *target*) domain adaptation settings *only*. In this paper, we propose a *semi-supervised*[1] (labeled data in *source*, and both labeled and unlabeled data in *target*) approach to leverage unlabeled data for EASYADAPT (which we call EA++) and empirically demonstrate its superior performance over EA as well as few other existing approaches.

There exists prior work on supervised domain adaptation (or multi-task learning) that can be related to EASYADAPT. An algorithm for multi-task learning using shared parameters was proposed (Evgeniou and Pontil, 2004) for multi-task regularization where each task parameter was represented as sum of a mean parameter (that stays same for all tasks) and its deviation from this mean. SVM was used as the base classifier and the algorithm was formulated in the standard SVM dual optimization setting. Subsequently, this framework (Evgeniou and Pontil, 2004) was extended (Dredze et al., 2010) to online multi-domain setting. Prior work on semi-supervised approaches to domain adaptation also exists in literature. Extraction of specific features from the available dataset was proposed (Arnold and Cohen, 2008; Blitzer et al., 2006) to facilitate the task of domain adaptation. Co-adaptation (Tur, 2009), a combination of co-training and domain adaptation, can also be considered as a semi-supervised approach to domain adaptation. A semi-supervised EM algorithm for domain adaptation was proposed in (Dai et al., 2007). Similar to graph based semi-supervised approaches, a label propagation method was proposed (Xing et al., 2007) to facilitate domain adaptation. The recently proposed Domain Adaptation Machine (DAM) (Duan et al., 2009) is a semi-supervised extension of SVMs for domain adaptation and presents extensive empirical results. However, in almost all of the above cases, the proposed methods either use specifics of the datasets or are customized for some particular base classifier and hence it is not clear how the proposed methods can be extended to other existing classifiers.

EA, on the other hand, is remarkably general in the sense that it can be used as a pre-processing

[1] We refer, labeled data in source and *only* unlabeled data in target, as the *unsupervised* domain adaptation setting.

Proceedings of the 2010 Workshop on Domain Adaptation for Natural Language Processing, ACL 2010, pages 53–59,
Uppsala, Sweden, 15 July 2010.

step in conjunction with any base classifier. However, one of the prime limitations of EA is its incapability to leverage unlabeled data. Given its simplicity and generality, it would be interesting to extend EA to semi-supervised settings. In this paper we propose EA++, a co-regularization based semi-supervised extension to EA. We present our approach and results for a single pair of source and target domain. However, we note that EA++ can also be extended to multiple source settings. If we have k sources and a single target domain then we can introduce a co-regularizer for each source-target pair. Due to space constraints, we defer details to a full version.

2 Background

2.1 Problem Setup and Notations

Let $\mathcal{X} \subset \mathbb{R}^d$ denote the instance space and $\mathcal{Y} = \{-1, +1\}$ denote the label space. We have a set of source labeled examples $L_s(\sim \mathcal{D}_s(x, y))$ and a set of target labeled examples $L_t(\sim \mathcal{D}_t(x, y))$, where $|L_s| = l_s \gg |L_t| = l_t$. We also have target unlabeled data denoted by $U_t(\sim \mathcal{D}_t(x))$, where $|U_t| = u_t$. Our goal is to learn a hypothesis $h : \mathcal{X} \mapsto \mathcal{Y}$ having low expected error with respect to the target domain. In this paper, we consider *linear hypotheses* only. However, the proposed techniques extend to non-linear hypotheses, as mentioned in (Daumé III, 2007). Source and target empirical errors for hypothesis h are denoted by $\hat{\epsilon}_s(h, f_s)$ and $\hat{\epsilon}_t(h, f_t)$ respectively, where f_s and f_t are source and target labeling functions. Similarly, the corresponding expected errors are denoted by $\epsilon_s(h, f_s)$ and $\epsilon_t(h, f_t)$. Shorthand notions of $\hat{\epsilon}_s$, $\hat{\epsilon}_t$, ϵ_s and ϵ_t have also been used.

2.2 EasyAdapt (EA)

In this section, we give a brief overview of EASYADAPT proposed in (Daumé III, 2007). Let us denote $\mathbb{R}^d$ as the *original* space. EA operates in an *augmented* space denoted by $\breve{\mathcal{X}} \subset \mathbb{R}^{3d}$ (for a single pair of source and target domain). For k domains, the *augmented* space blows up to $\mathbb{R}^{(k+1)d}$. The augmented feature maps $\Phi^s, \Phi^t : \mathcal{X} \mapsto \breve{\mathcal{X}}$ for source and target domains are defined as,

$$\begin{aligned} \Phi^s(\mathbf{x}) &= \langle \mathbf{x}, \mathbf{x}, \mathbf{0} \rangle \\ \Phi^t(\mathbf{x}) &= \langle \mathbf{x}, \mathbf{0}, \mathbf{x} \rangle \end{aligned} \tag{2.1}$$

where $\mathbf{x}$ and $\mathbf{0}$ are vectors in $\mathbb{R}^d$, and $\mathbf{0}$ denotes a zero vector of dimension d. The first d-dimensional segment corresponds to commonality between source and target, second d-dimensional segment corresponds to the source domain while the last segment corresponds to the target domain. Source and target domain features are transformed using these feature maps and the augmented feature space so constructed is passed onto the underlying supervised classifier. One of the most appealing properties of EASYADAPT is that it is agnostic of the underlying supervised classifier being used to learn in the *augmented* space. Almost any *standard supervised learning approach for linear classifiers* (for e.g., SVMs, perceptrons) can be used to learn a *linear hypothesis* $\breve{\mathbf{h}} \in \mathbb{R}^{3d}$ in the augmented space. As mentioned earlier, this work considers linear hypotheses only and the the proposed techniques can be extended (Daumé III, 2007) to non-linear hypotheses. Let us denote $\breve{\mathbf{h}} = \langle \mathbf{h_c}, \mathbf{h_s}, \mathbf{h_t} \rangle$, where each of $\mathbf{h_c}$, $\mathbf{h_s}$, $\mathbf{h_t}$ is of dimension d and represent the *common*, *source-specific* and *target-specific* components of $\breve{\mathbf{h}}$, respectively. During prediction on target data, the incoming target feature $\mathbf{x}$ is transformed to obtain $\Phi^t(\mathbf{x})$ and $\breve{\mathbf{h}}$ is applied on this transformed feature. This is equivalent to applying $(\mathbf{h_c} + \mathbf{h_t})$ on $\mathbf{x}$.

A good intuitive insight into why this simple algorithm works so well in practice and outperforms most state-of-the-art algorithms is given in (Daumé III, 2007). Briefly, it can be thought to be simultaneously training two hypotheses: $\mathbf{w_s} = (\mathbf{h_c} + \mathbf{h_s})$ for source domain and $\mathbf{w_t} = (\mathbf{h_c} + \mathbf{g_t})$ for target domain. The commonality between the domains is represented by $\mathbf{h_c}$ whereas the source and target domain specific information is captured by $\mathbf{h_s}$ and $\mathbf{h_t}$, respectively. This technique can be easily extended to a multi-domain scenario by making more copies of the original feature space ($(K+1)$ copies in case of K domains). A kernelized version of the algorithm has also been presented in (Daumé III, 2007).

3 Using Unlabeled data

As discussed in the previous section, the EASYADAPT algorithm is attractive because it performs very well empirically and can be used in conjunction with any underlying supervised classifier. One drawback of EASYADAPT is that it does not make use of unlabeled target data which is generally available in large quantity in most practical problems. In this section, we propose a semi-supervised extension of this algorithm while maintaining the desirable classifier-agnostic property.

3.1 Motivation

In multi-view approach for semi-supervised learning algorithms (Sindhwani et al., 2005), different hypotheses are learned in different *views*. Thereafter, unlabeled data is utilized to co-regularize these learned hypotheses by making them agree on unlabeled samples. In domain adaptation, the source and target data come from two different distributions. However, if the source and target domains are *reasonably close* to each other, we can employ a similar form of regularization using unlabeled data. A similar co-regularizer based approach for unlabeled data was previously shown (Duan et al., 2009) to give improved empirical results for domain adaptation task. However, their technique applies for the particular base classifier they consider and hence does not extend to EASYADAPT.

3.2 EA++: EASYADAPT with unlabeled data

In our proposed semi-supervised extension to EASYADAPT, the source and target hypothesis are made to agree on unlabeled data. We refer to this algorithm as EA++. Recall that EASYADAPT learns a linear hypothesis $\breve{\mathbf{h}} \in \mathbb{R}^{3d}$ in the *augmented* space. The hypothesis $\breve{\mathbf{h}}$ contains common, source and target sub-hypotheses and is expressed as $\breve{\mathbf{h}} = \langle \mathbf{h_c}, \mathbf{h_s}, \mathbf{h_t} \rangle$. In *original* space (ref. section 2.2), this is equivalent to learning a source specific hypothesis $\mathbf{w_s} = (\mathbf{h_c} + \mathbf{h_s})$ and a target specific hypothesis $\mathbf{w_t} = (\mathbf{h_c} + \mathbf{h_t})$.

In EA++, we want source hypothesis $\mathbf{w_s}$ and target hypothesis $\mathbf{w_t}$ to agree on unlabeled data. For some unlabeled target sample $\mathbf{x_i} \in \mathcal{U}_t \subset \mathbb{R}^d$, EA++ would implicitly want to make the predictions of $\mathbf{w_t}$ and $\mathbf{w_t}$ on $\mathbf{x_i}$ to agree. Formally, it aims to achieve the following condition:

$$\begin{aligned} & \mathbf{w_s} \cdot \mathbf{x_i} \approx \mathbf{w_t} \cdot \mathbf{x_i} \\ \iff & (\mathbf{h_c} + \mathbf{h_s}) \cdot \mathbf{x_i} \approx (\mathbf{h_c} + \mathbf{h_t}) \cdot \mathbf{x_i} \\ \iff & (\mathbf{h_s} - \mathbf{h_t}) \cdot \mathbf{x_i} \approx 0 \\ \iff & \langle \mathbf{h_c}, \mathbf{h_s}, \mathbf{h_t} \rangle \cdot \langle \mathbf{0}, \mathbf{x_i}, -\mathbf{x_i} \rangle \approx 0. \end{aligned} \tag{3.1}$$

We define another feature map $\Phi^u : X \mapsto \breve{X}$ for unlabeled data as below:

$$\Phi^u(\mathbf{x}) = \langle \mathbf{0}, \mathbf{x}, -\mathbf{x} \rangle. \tag{3.2}$$

Every unlabeled sample is transformed using the map $\Phi^u(.)$. The augmented feature space that results from the application of three feature maps, namely, $\Phi^s : X \mapsto \breve{X}, \Phi^t : X \mapsto \breve{X}, \Phi^u : X \mapsto \breve{X}$, on source labeled samples, target labeled sampled and target unlabeled samples is summarized in Figure 1.

As shown in Eq. 3.1, during the training phase, EA++ assigns a predicted value close to 0 for each unlabeled sample. However, it is worth noting that, during the test phase, EA++ predicts labels from two classes: $+1$ and -1. This warrants further exposition of the implementation specifics which is deferred until the next subsection.

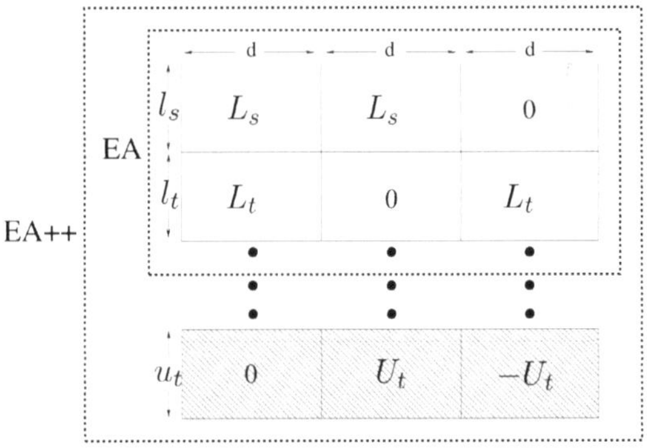

Figure 1: Diagrammatic representation of feature augmentation in EA and EA++

Algorithm 1 presents the EA++ approach in detail.

3.3 Implementation

In this section, we present implementation specific details of EA++. We consider SVM as our base supervised learner ($\mathcal{LEARN}$ in Algorithm 1). However, these details hold for other supervised

Algorithm 1 EA++

Input: L_s; L_t; U_t; $\mathcal{LEARN}$: supervised classifier

Output: $\breve{h}$: classifier learned in augmented space

/* initialize augmented training set */

1: $P := \{\}$

/* construct augmented training set */

2: $\forall(\mathbf{x}, y) \in L_s, P := P \cup \{\Phi^s(\mathbf{x}), y\}$

3: $\forall(\mathbf{x}, y) \in L_t, P := P \cup \{\Phi^t(\mathbf{x}), y\}$

4: $\forall\mathbf{x} \in U_t, P := P \cup \{\Phi^u(\mathbf{x}), 0\}$

/* output learned classifier */

5: $\breve{h} = \mathcal{LEARN}(P)$

classifiers too. In the dual form of SVM optimization function, the labels are multiplied with the inner product of features. This can make the unlabeled samples redundant since we want their labels to be 0 according to Eq. 3.1. To avoid this, we create as many copies of $\Phi^u(\mathbf{x})$ as there are labels and assign each label to one copy. For the case of binary classification, we create two copies of every augmented unlabeled sample, and assign $+1$ label to one copy and -1 to the other. The learner attempts to balance the loss of the two copies, and tries to make the prediction on unlabeled sample equal to 0. Figure 2 shows the curves of the hinge loss for class $+1$, class -1 and their sum. The effective loss for each unlabeled sample is similar to the sum of losses for $+1$ and -1 classes (shown in Figure 2c).

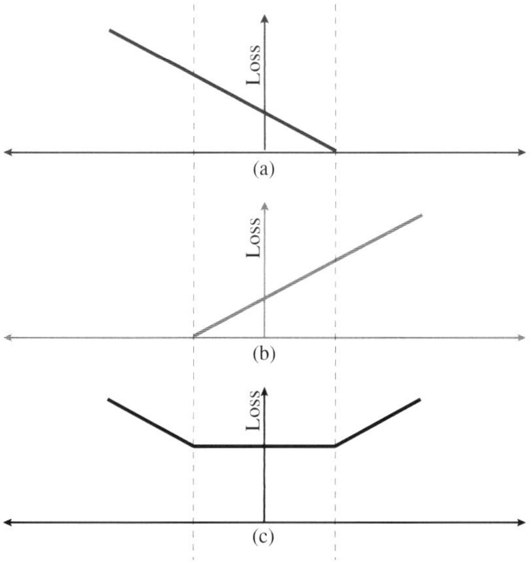

Figure 2: Loss functions for class $+1$, class -1 and unlabeled samples.

4 Experiments

In this section, we demonstrate the empirical performance of EA augmented with unlabeled data.

4.1 Setup

We follow the same experimental setup used in (Daumé III, 2007) and perform two sequence labelling tasks (a) named-entity-recognition (NER), and (b) part-of-speech-tagging (POS)on the following datasets:

PubMed-POS: Introduced by (Blitzer et al., 2006), this dataset consists of two domains. The WSJ portion of the Penn Treebank serves as the source domain and the PubMed abstracts serve as the target domain. The task is to perform part-of-speech tagging on unlabeled PubMed abstracts with a classifier trained on labeled WSJ and PubMed data.

Treebank-Brown. Treebank-Chunk data consists of the following domains: the standard WSJ domain (the same data as for CoNLL 2000), the ATIS switchboard domain and the Brown corpus. The Brown corpus consists of data combined from six subdomains. Treebank-Chunk is a shallow parsing task based on the data from the Penn Treebank. Treebank-Brown is identical to the Treebank-Chunk task, However, in Treebank-Brown we consider all of the Brown corpus to be a single domain.

Table 1 presents a summary of the datasets used. All datasets use roughly the same feature set which are lexical information (words, stems, capitalization, prefixes and suffixes), membership on gazetteers, etc. We use an averaged perceptron classifier from the Megam framework (implementation due to (Daumé III, 2004)) for all the aforementioned tasks. The training sample size varies from $1k$ to $16k$. In all cases, the amount of unlabeled target data was equal to the total amount of labeled source and target data.

Task	Dom	#Tr	#De	#Te	#Ft
PubMed	src	950,028	-	-	571k
POS	tgt	11,264	1,987	14,554	39k
	wsj	191,209	29,455	38,440	94k
	swbd3	45,282	5,596	41,840	55k
	br-cf	58,201	8,307	7,607	144k
Tree	br-cg	67,429	9,444	6,897	149k
bank-	br-ck	51,379	6,061	9,451	121k
Chunk	br-cl	47,382	5,101	5,880	95k
	br-cm	11,696	1,324	1,594	51k
	br-cn	56,057	6,751	7,847	115k
	br-cp	55,318	7,477	5,977	112k
	br-cr	16,742	2,522	2,712	65k

Table 1: Summary of Datasets. The columns denote task, domain, size of training, development and test data sets, and the number of unique features in the training data.

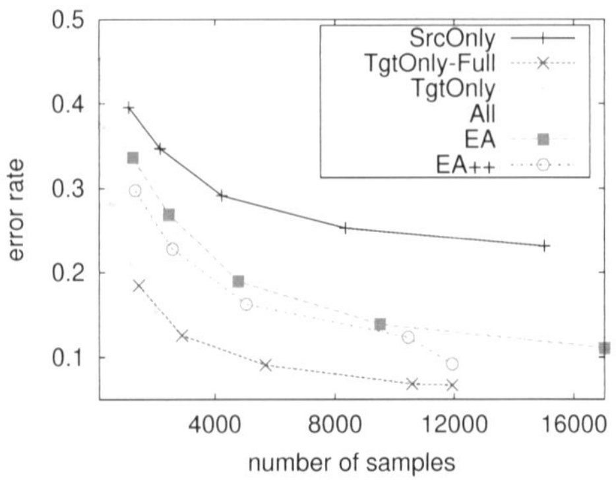

(a)

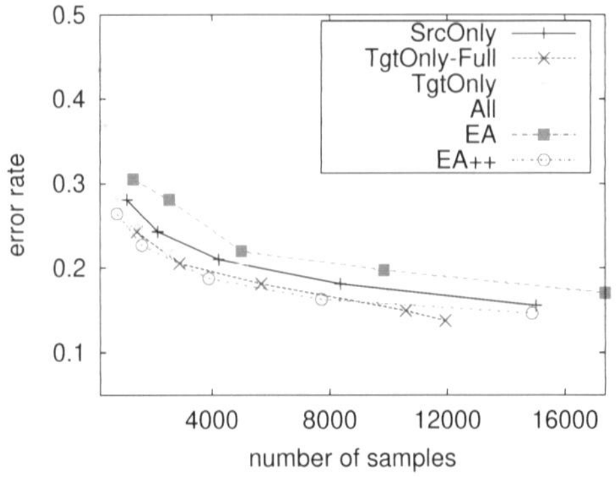

(b)

Figure 3: Test accuracy of (a) PubMed-POS and (b) Treebank-Brown for, SOURCEONLY, TARGETONLY-FULL, TARGETONLY, ALL, EA and EA++.

4.2 Results

We compare the empirical performance of EA++ with a few other baselines, namely, (a) SOURCEONLY (classifier trained on source labeled samples), (b) TARGETONLY-FULL (classifier trained on the same number of target labeled samples as the number of source labeled samples in SOURCEONLY), (c) TARGETONLY (classifier trained on small amount of target labeled samples, roughly one-tenth of the amount of source labeled samples in SOURCEONLY), (d) ALL (classifier trained on combined labeled samples of SOURCEONLY and TARGETONLY), (e) EA (classifier trained in *augmented feature space* on the same input training set as ALL), (f) EA++ (classifier trained in *augmented feature space* on the same input training set as EA and an equal amount of unlabeled *target* data). All these approaches were tested on the entire amount of available *target* test data.

Figure 3 presents the learning curves for (a) SOURCEONLY, (b) TARGETONLY-FULL, (c) TARGETONLY, (d) ALL, (e) EA, and (f) EA++ (EA with unlabeled data). The x-axis represents the number of training samples on which the predictor has been trained. At this point, we note that the number of training samples vary depending on the particular approach being used. For SOURCEONLY, TARGETONLY-FULL and TARGETONLY, it is just the corresponding number of labeled source or target samples, respectively. For ALL and EA, it is the summation of labeled source and target samples. For EA++, the x-value plotted denotes the amount of unlabeled target data used (in addition to an equal amount of source+target labeled data, as in ALL or EA). We plot this number for EA++, just to compare its improvement over EA when using an additional (and equal) amount of unlabeled target data. This accounts for the different x values plotted for the different curves. In all cases, the y-axis denotes the error rate.

As can be seen in Figure 3(a), EA++ performs better than the normal EA (which uses labeled data only). The labeled and unlabeled case start together but with increase in number of samples their gap increases with the unlabeled case resulting in much lower error as compared to the labeled case. Similar trends were observed in other data sets as can be seen in Figure 3(b). We also note that EA performs poorly for some cases, as was shown (Daumé III, 2007) earlier.

5 Summary

In this paper, we have proposed a semi-supervised extension to an existing domain adaptation technique (EA). Our approach EA++, leverages the unlabeled data to improve the performance of EA. Empirical results demonstrate improved accuracy for sequential labeling tasks performed on standardized datasets. The previously proposed EA could be applied exclusively to *fully supervised* domain adaptation problems only. However, with the current extension, EA++ applies to both *fully supervised* and *semi-supervised* domain adaptation problems.

6 Future Work

In both EA and EA++, we use features from source and target space to construct an augmented feature space. In other words, we are sharing features across source and target *labeled* data. We term such algorithms as *Feature Sharing Algorithms*. Feature sharing algorithms are effective for domain adaptation because they are simple, easy to implement as a preprocessing step and outperform many existing state-of-the-art techniques (shown previously for domain adaptation (Daumé III, 2007)). However, despite their simplicity and empirical success, it is not theoretically apparent why these algorithms perform so well. Prior work provides some intuitions but is mostly empirical and a formal theoretical analysis to justify FSAs (for domain adaptation) is clearly missing. Prior work (Maurer, 2006) analyzes the multi-task regularization approach (Evgeniou and Pontil, 2004) (which is related to EA) but they consider a cumulative loss in multi-task (or multi-domain) setting. This does not apply to domain adaptation setting where we are mainly interested in loss in the target domain *only*.

Theoretically analyzing the superior performance of EA and EA++ and providing generalization guarantees is an interesting line of future work. One approach would be to model the feature sharing approach in terms of co-regularization; an idea that originated in the context of multiview learning and for which some theoretical analysis has already been done (Rosenberg and Bartlett, 2007; Sindhwani and Rosenberg, 2008). Additionally, the aforementioned techniques, namely, SOURCEONLY, TARGETONLY, ALL have been empirically compared to EA and EA++. It would be interesting to formally frame these approaches and see whether their empirical performance can be justified within a theoretical framework.

References

Andrew Arnold and William W. Cohen. 2008. Intra-document structural frequency features for semi-supervised domain adaptation. In *CIKM'08*, pages 1291–1300, Napa Valley, California, USA.

John Blitzer, Ryan Mcdonald, and Fernando Pereira. 2006. Domain adaptation with structural correspondence learning. In *EMNLP'06*, pages 120–128, Sydney, Australia.

Wenyuan Dai, Gui-Rong Xue, Qiang Yang, and Yong Yu. 2007. Transferring Naive Bayes classifiers for text classification. In *AAAI'07*, pages 540–545, Vancouver, B.C.

Hal Daumé III. 2004. Notes on CG and LM-BFGS optimization of logistic regression. August.

Hal Daumé III. 2007. Frustratingly easy domain adaptation. In *ACL'07*, pages 256–263, Prague, Czech Republic.

Mark Dredze, Alex Kulesza, and Koby Crammer. 2010. Multi-domain learning by confidence-weighted parameter combination. *Machine Learning*, 79.

Lixin Duan, Ivor W. Tsang, Dong Xu, and Tat-Seng Chua. 2009. Domain adaptation from multiple sources via auxiliary classifiers. In *ICML'09*, pages 289–296, Montreal, Quebec.

Theodoros Evgeniou and Massimiliano Pontil. 2004. Regularized multitask learning. In *KDD'04*, pages 109–117, Seattle, WA, USA.

Andreas Maurer. 2006. The Rademacher complexity of linear transformation classes. In *COLT'06*, pages 65–78, Pittsburgh, Pennsylvania.

D. S. Rosenberg and P. L. Bartlett. 2007. The Rademacher complexity of co-regularized kernel classes. In *AISTATS'07*, San Juan, Puerto Rico.

Vikas Sindhwani and David S. Rosenberg. 2008. An RKHS for multi-view learning and manifold co-regularization. In *ICML'08*, pages 976–983, Helsinki, Finland.

Vikas Sindhwani, Partha Niyogi, and Mikhail Belkin. 2005. A co-regularization approach to semi-supervised learning with multiple views. In *ICML Workshop on Learning with Multiple Views*, pages 824–831, Bonn, Germany.

Gokhan Tur. 2009. Co-adaptation: Adaptive co-training for semi-supervised learning. In *ICASSP'09*, pages 3721–3724, Taipei, Taiwan.

Dikan Xing, Wenyuan Dai, Gui-Rong Xue, and Yong Yu. 2007. Bridged refinement for transfer learning. In *PKDD'07*, pages 324–335, Warsaw, Poland.

Author Index